T0345221

A Skeleton Plays Violin

THE GERMAN LIST

GEORG TRAKL

A Skeleton Plays Violin

THE EARLY, UNPUBLISHED AND LAST WORKS OF GEORG TRAKL

Book Three of Our Trakl

TRANSLATED BY JAMES REIDEL

Seagull
BOOKS

LONDON NEW YORK CALCUTTA

GOETHE INSTITUT

This publication was supported by a grant from
the Goethe-Institut India

Grateful acknowledgment is made to the following publications
in which some of these translations originally appeared: *Battersea
Review* for 'Delirium'; *Map Literary* for 'Something pale, lying in
the shadows of a falling staircase' 'The stillness of the departed
loves the old garden', 'With pink steps the stone descends into
the moor', 'The blue night has softly risen on our foreheads' and
'O living in the stillness of the darkening garden'; *Mudlark* for
'At the Rim of an Old Fountain', 'Melancholy', 'To Angela', 'To
Johanna', 'To Slacken' and 'To Lucifer'; and *Verse* for 'Barabbas',
'Mary Magdalene', 'Neglect' and 'Revelation and Perdition'.

Seagull Books, 2017

Translation © James Reidel, 2017

ISBN 978 0 8574 2 429 7

British Cataloguing-in-Publication Data
A catalogue record for this book is available
from the British Library

Typeset in Adobe Caslon Pro by Seagull Books, Calcutta, India
Printed and bound at Maple Press, York, Pennsylvania, USA

Contents

Translator's Note

In any foreign country I would
read you, or at home too
Robert Walser, 'To Georg Trakl'

Trakl, con the male nurse.
Surmounted by carrion cry out and overdose & go.
John Berryman, 'Drugs Alcohol Little Sister'

This book is the third and final volume in a series I call *Our Trakl*. This overarching title recognizes something both universal and personal in that the Austrian poet Georg Trakl belongs in the canon of world literature. In that sense he is 'ours'. However, because of the way his poetry is apprehended individually—that we each hear and apprehend Trakl differently—he is 'ours' as individuals, too.

When I began to write poems in the late 1970s, I had the good fortune of befriending two younger poets who had already encountered Trakl—Daniel Simko and Franz

Wright. Franz's father, James, with the poet Robert Bly, had published a chapbook of their translations of Trakl's poems, one of the first in English and owing some of its impetus to the revival of interest in Trakl in Austria and Germany following the Nazi period. This chapbook became one of my prized possessions and it surely influenced my work and my ideas about culture and history, serving as the moral antithesis to another Austrian of his generation, Adolf Hitler.

I remember trying to get one of my poems published in *Ironwood*, a journal that was much respected by my peers. The first poem I placed was an homage to Trakl, having encountered his work initially in a room lit by a black-and-white television and in a world far removed from his. But the difference was a matter of setting—my world in Ohio and Cincinnati felt much like a strange province of the fading empire evoked in Trakl's work.

Later, when I had moved to New York City to work and attend graduate school at Columbia, I witnessed first-hand the need and difficulty of translating Trakl's poetry. Daniel Simko had been struggling with a selection that he eventually published with the title *Autumn Sonata* (1989). I believe this was the first translated work since Jonathan Cape published a small selection translated by Michael Hamburger and colleagues in 1968. For me, Trakl coexisted in the background with my interest in the American poet Weldon Kees who was born in same year that Trakl died. And Trakl's father and Kees' both made their fortunes in metal hardware. And I was born in 1955, when Kees disappeared for ever. If nothing else, the coincidental dates stoked my affinity for both poets' work. Whatever the clockwork, it did not go unnoticed by John Berryman, also born in 1914. He notes the same symmetry in the poem which provides my second epigraph, that when he 'peered' from the womb, Trakl 'had [only] nine nights to spare'.

Over time, I read (and translated) my way back to Trakl in the works of postwar writers Thomas Bernhard and Ingeborg Bachmann and Trakl's Expressionist contemporary, Franz Werfel. Meanwhile, new translations of Trakl's poems appeared, each one adding to the various shades of meaning, how one could be careful with a verse or push it to where Trakl meant it *univocally*, despite, as Heidegger puts it, its *mehrdeutig* quality, its multiplicity of meaning, its ambiguous ambiguity which the philosopher praised as 'peerless'.

In this spirit, which I liken to climbing a glass mountain wherein some enchanted personage lives for ever, I have added *my Trakl*. I have done so by rendering his first two books, *Poems* (*Gedichte*, 1913) and *Sebastian Dreaming* (*Sebastian im Traum*, 1915), as the discrete and inviolable productions he intended. For a selection, omitting poems would damage the whole of either book—and to gather them into a collected volume would overwhelm the integrity of their presentation, their reading experience, their desired effect. This third volume, however, is not simply a *Nachlass*—a literary legacy, a collection of juvenilia, unpublished work and so on. These poems and prose pieces suggest the ghosts of other books, hauntologies of books as it were, that in one place reveal Trakl's development, maturity and where he intended to go had he survived himself and the First World War. To achieve this, *everything* in the collected German editions is not here, just the most significant examples of *everything* are, interpolated with a long, critical biographical note that aggregates what I know and think about Trakl.

This leads me to the third way Trakl is ours. Whoever reads his work unavoidably will speculate where his story and his verse overlap and ponder the presence of the sister (the princess in Trakl's glass mountain). In seeing what we want to see—a kind of ideal and unattainable being, the infamous allegations of incest—that have resulted in not only scholarly books but also a novel and a costume drama—we really are using pieces that have to be forced. So, in presenting the work here chronologically, I have pressed a few of my own together, seeing Trakl as I see him, someone who wanted to be a liminal being in this world and the next.

Sources and Organization

For all three volumes of *Our Trakl*, I have used *Dichtungen und Briefe* (Poems and Letters), 2nd edn (Salzburg: Otto Müller Verlag, 1987), indeed, from the two-volume set that once belonged to Daniel Simko—hence my sentimental reasons for using it over the 'Innsbruck edition' edited by Zwerschina and Sauermann. Over the years, I have been an aggregator of readings and conversations with others about Trakl's life, his critical reception and the various legends attached to him and his sister Grete Trakl. Ultimately, though, much of what I know about Trakl originates with Gebhard Rusch and Siegfried J. Schmidt, *Das Voraussetzungssystem Georg Trakls* (A Systematic Understanding of Georg Trakl) (Wiesbaden, Germany: Springer, 1983). Hans Weichselbaum's critical biography, *Georg Trakl* (Salzburg: Otto Müller, 1994), is also an invaluable source for anyone writing about Trakl and his work. For the life of Grete Trakl, I relied on Marty Bax's biography, *Immer zu wenig Liebe—Grete Trakl. Ihr feinster Kuppler. Ihre Familie.* (Always Too Little Love: Grete Trakl, Her Fine Procurer and Family) (Amsterdam: Bax Art, 2015) and Charles Chiu's 'Margarete Jeanne Trakl' in *Women in the Shadows* (New York: Peter Lang, 2008). Another valuable source is the Ludwig von Ficker's *Briefwechsel* (Correspondence), *1909–1914* and *1915–1925* (Salzburg: Otto Müller, 1986, 1988).

In addition to my endnotes, a biographical note is interpolated between the parts of the third volume of *Our Trakl* and complements the organization of his uncollected works in an approximately chronological fashion. The first and final parts are devoted to his early and late published works, and brace what can be read as an unpublished early book, the 'Collation of 1909'. With very few omissions, the second and third parts are what I feel to be judicious selection of finished poems, variants and derivations—that is, the working manuscripts from which that Trakl drew the poems for his two published books, *Poems* and *Sebastian Dreaming*, and saw a third that this book can only suggest.

Published Prose and Poetry, 1906–1909

. . . I surely worked a good deal. To get over the subsequent strain on my nerves, I have unfortunately resorted to chloroform. The effect was awful.

Georg Trakl to Karl von Kalmar, August–September 1905

'He has assiduously read Ibsen, taken on Nietzsche,' wrote one theatre critic after the April 1906 premiere of Trakl's lost one-act play *Totentag*—and debut. 'Literarily ambitious, his young breast full of ideals, Trakl experiments with an abundance of thoughts, ideas, motivations, which his aforementioned readings have imposed on him, dressing them in his own clothes'. *Totentag*—Day of the Dead, All Soul's Day—is set in the late autumn. According to the play's program, a 'philosophical blind young man' named Peter Asmus comes to the realization that 'only the child can believe in the Bible, but not the man'. He longs for the joy of life which is closed to him but open in every way for his younger sister. He is a seer who sees all that his sister will do in life. Before the curtain falls, the blind Peter pulling out a revolver, aiming it, and then putting it away, saying, 'Don't play with firearms, for you will feel the pain.' What else is known of the play can be found in a review, where it is apparent that Peter loves his sister Grete, but he sees her future marriage destroying what little happiness he knows. He makes plans to kill her before he is 'entirely alone'. But his sinister plan—or fantasy—is only frustrated by the timely appearance of her bridegroom.

Another dramatic scene, also lost, appeared on the Salzburg stage later in the autumn of the same year. The critics saw a new Hofmannsthal and Maeterlinck in *Fata Morgana*, a play in which another young man, a 'son of the desert', one sunburnt by the life of the shepherd or goatherd, speaks to its unattainable symbol— Cleopatra, still a young princess but a mirage enthroned on an isolated rock. The play was noted for its blend of the Old Testament, fairy tales, philosophy and mysticism.

Despite these accomplishments—the critics also knew of his praiseworthy prose works in the feuilletons of Salzburg's newspapers—Trakl wrote to a friend that he had hardly written anything for a long time.

Georg Trakl was born on 3 February 1887, to an upper-middle-class family living in the archbishopric and provincial capital of Salzburg, one of the major cities of the Austro-Hungarian Empire. His father, Tobias Trakl, born in the Swabian German town of Ödenburg (now Sopron) in Hungary, established him-self as a successful hardware retailer in the 1860s, a period in Central European history called the *Gründerzeit*, that 'time of the founding' of many of the German and Austrian industrial companies and corporations.

Tobias had lost his first wife Valentine shortly after she gave birth to his son Wilhelm—'Willy'—in 1868. A few years later, in 1875, Tobias married again, a young Viennese woman of

Czech ancestry, Maria Halik. Their firstborn, Gustav, was born in 1879 and died a year later. Their second son, also named Gustav, was born in 1880; then two daughters, Maria ('Mia', 1882) and Hermina ('Mina', 1884); then Georg in 1887; then younger siblings, Friedrich ('Fritz', 1890) and Margarete Jeanne ('Gretl' or 'Grete', 1891).

Tobias' firm grew as well as his family, compelling him to move several times until the Trakls were ensconced in a roomy house at Waagplatz 3 in Salzburg's Old City, the site of a Roman villa whose floor mosaics were buried under the foundation. The antiquity of Georg's birthplace was complemented by his mother's collection of family heirlooms and antique furniture; she devoted herself more to them than her house full of children, quite possibly to cope with post-partum depression and the burden of caring for so many young. Thus, befitting her status as a woman of the *Bürgertum*, the *haute bourgeoisie*, Maria relied on wet nurses and caretakers, the most important of these being Marie Boring, the Alsatian French governess Tobias hired in 1890 to care for his five children and the new baby.

The pedagogy that Mlle Boring employed on Trakl and his siblings over the next fifteen years required that they become fluent in French as well as German. Their lessons in art, arithmetic, reading and similar subjects were conducted partly in French, and the children were encouraged to speak French to one another. The only part of their education that Frau Trakl oversaw was their piano lessons, at which Georg and later his youngest sister, Grete, excelled.

Mlle Boring was also a staunch Catholic and this led to a religious conflict with her employers, who feared that she might try to convert her charges (perhaps rightly given the Catholic imagery found in Trakl's work). After an argument over the children's religious upbringing, Mlle Boring left the family for almost two years before agreeing to return and fill the void Frau Trakl had been unwilling to fill herself, preferring the isolation of her quarters in the Trakl house, where it was 'Tabu' for the children to enter without permission. Nevertheless, as long as the children remained by their doting father and loving French governess whom they adored, they—including Georg during his early years—felt happy and whole. The hardware business, however, took up much of Tobias' time (as did the Austrian passion for cards—his favourite game being Tarot). To compensate—and so that his wife might not be disturbed by their voices—Tobias purchased a forested garden lot where his children could be taken to play. It had a fountain and a small, enclosed gazebo—a *Salettl*—built for make-believe games, and Georg spent much time here with his siblings and its effect on his imagination is telling and redolent of a lost and happier world and time.

That Georg was different from his brothers and sisters became more apparent even before he started school. At the age of five, he walked or fell into a pond, an event ascribed to 'absent-mindedness' but perhaps his first known attempt at suicide. He also tried to throw himself in front of a horse-drawn tram. Otherwise, he seemed to be just a shy, healthy and physically normal boy who thrived best in the company of his sister Grete, whose striking resemblance to him increased with each year. Grete was the only child her mother nursed, and who grew up spoiled as the family favourite given her talent at the keyboard. To her parents, it seemed as though she might be a musical prodigy—like Mozart, whose monument in Salzburg could be seen from the windows of her father's main shop. Georg, being a middle child, proved to be Grete's defender and reconciler when her imperiousness got her into petty arguments with her sisters. For her part, she relished his attentions and loyalty.

In 1897, Trakl passed the requisite examinations for public high school (*Staatsgymnasium*). There, however, he proved to be withdrawn and something of a loner. His classmates saw him as an outsider, whose usual facial expression was a silent, obstinate sneer and who was most often hunched over his desk or sitting like a statue, his nose and its flared nostrils buried in one hand. While he could be off-putting, Trakl's demeanour and knowledge of Dostoevsky attracted other nonconformists, such as his close friend, the writer and caricaturist Erhard Buschbeck. For them, Trakl was always a person of interest—even to the Chinese pen pal he cultivated in the artificial language of Volapük, which, if it did not have some influence on his poetry, suggests his intense diligence with his own language, as though every word had been carefully looked up in many dictionaries.

The descriptions of Trakl's behaviours—together with the fixations and extreme intellect in his poetry—would one day come under the scrutiny of the Austrian paediatrician Hans Asperger, who saw the poet as a possible victim of the syndrome that bears his name. And, indeed, like a classic example of one who exhibits this spectrum of autism, Trakl's grades suffered during those years which saw the turn of the century, and he was forced to repeat the fourth and seventh grades. The rigors of the latter perhaps resulted in him leaving school for a time and being sent to relatives in Ödenburg, where he recovered from a bout of nervous exhaustion—an event that inspired his prose piece 'Dreamland'.

Meanwhile, Trakl's self-education continued and compensated for the drills and rote that left him distracted and detached. Under the care of Mlle Boring, he had shown a special interest in French poetry and read Baudelaire, Rimbaud and Verlaine. In addition to the novels of Dostoyevsky, he read and attended plays by Maeterlinck and Hofmannsthal. He also loved the poems of Nicholas Lenau and Friedrich Hölderlin, a Romantic poet whose rediscovery in the early years of the twentieth century would have a profound effect on German Expressionism.

In 1905, Trakl left high school without earning a diploma. This, of course, limited him in what vocation to choose, for he did not want to enter the family business, where 'Willy'—the adult half-brother—would be his superior, a half-brother who had little sympathy for an aspiring poet. Still, Georg, needing to choose a respectable middle-class vocation, took a position as an apprentice pharmacist at the Zum weißen Engel—the White Angel—in Salzburg, whose name implied the mercies it afforded in various medications and painkillers. That his father allowed him to embark on such a career is surprising, given yet another of Georg's near-death experiences when he had been found in his room unconscious from inhaling chloroform. Although in this he had simply imitated his mother, who used the drug to calm her nerves, Trakl's addictions were hardly innocent; he had been inhaling chloroform and smoking cigarettes laced with opium since the age of fourteen, if not earlier, and would graduate to Veronal, and cocaine, easily found at his new job. That he could still write, and write well, points to the high-functioning addict who existed alongside the disciplined artist.

The young Trakl did not need the example of his mother—taking drugs went with being a poet as did rebelling against anything petty bourgeois; and being a libertine, the teenage Trakl became a client of Salzburg's various houses of ill repute. He had written his first poems by the age of fifteen, and befriended a small coterie of young nonconformists with a literary bent who gathered at the Café Tomaselli and gave their circle an appropriately pagan name, first 'Apollo' and then 'Minerva'. But even among them he was seen as an outsider's outsider. An inveterate walker—a *Spaziergänger*—he more often went alone and mixed this healthful activity with inhaling chloroform and being found insensible on a park bench. His appearance and stare could be disturbing in its intensity. He did not take criticism well and often withdrew over it, feeling dissatisfied with himself and his work. His defence mechanism was to reject it and move on to a new work which would be perfect—a pattern, too, that only changed in its particulars.

Despite himself, Trakl worked hard at the White Angel. He also began to write the mature plays and prose he published throughout 1906 before the lyric poems he also began to write during his youth in Salzburg, as he moved away from those efforts inspired by first love, first passion, with their unsettled and abstract objects of desire which hardly resemble Grete.

Throughout the late 1890s and early 1900s, Grete was often far from the orbit and influence of her notorious brother, attending Catholic boarding schools where she continued her piano studies. She would seem only to be in the same picture with him when they were photographed together as very young children. Nevertheless, when he published, Grete was in her fifteenth year and old enough to be impressed by her brother's accomplishment. She too would have been one of his first readers, and doing so would begin to make up for the time they were kept apart.

Dreamland

An Episode

Sometimes I have to think of those silent days again that are to me like a wondrously, happily spent life which I undoubtedly enjoyed like a gift from generous, unknown hands. And once more that small town in the valley stood there in my memory, with its broad main avenue, through which a long alley of splendid linden trees ran, with its angular side streets, filled with the secret, profitable lives of petty merchants and artisans—and with the old town fountain in the middle of the square, which splashed so dreamily in the sunshine, and where, with evening, the water's whispers of love begin to rush. But then the town itself seems to dream of some past life.

And gently rolling hills stretch out above the solemn, silent pine forests, closing off the valley from the outside world. The peaks softly nestle against the far, clear skies, and with this contact of heaven and earth some of that world above seems to be a part of this homeland. Human shapes come to mind all at once and before me their past lives come to life again, with all their little sorrows and joys, which these people could confide among each other without trepidation.

I lived in this remoteness for eight weeks; these eight weeks are like a separate, distinct part of my life to me—a life unto itself—full of an inexpressible, youthful happiness, full of a strong desire for distant, beautiful things. Here, for the first time, my juvenile soul received this impression of some great experience.

I see myself again as a schoolboy in this little house a short way outside the town, with a small garden in front almost entirely hidden by trees and shrubs. There I lived in a small attic room, decorated with quaint, old faded pictures, and sometimes during the evening I dreamt there in the stillness, and the stillness lovingly recorded and stored my sky-high, foolishly happy juvenile dreams into itself and often enough replayed them for me later—during the lonely hours of twilight. Often too, in the evening, I came downstairs to my old uncle who spent nearly the whole day with his sick daughter Maria. Then we three sat silently together for hours at a time. The warm evening wind blew inside the window and carried all kinds of muddled sounds to our ears, which made one see these obscure visions. And the air was filled with the strong, heady smell of the roses which bloomed along the garden fence.

Slowly the night crept into the room and then I stood up, said 'Good night' and took myself upstairs to my room to dream there for an hour longer at the window, into the night outside.

Initially, I felt something, like being oppressed with fear, after being so close to that sick little girl, which later changed to a holy, reverential awe before this strange, mute and poignant sorrow. When I saw her, a dark feeling rose inside me, that she would have to die. And then I was afraid to look at her.

Through the course of the day, when I roamed the forests, feeling so happy in the solitude and stillness, when I stretched out tired on the moss and for hours at a time stared into the clear, shimmering sky in which one could see so far, when a deep strange feeling of happiness intoxicated me, the thought of the sick Maria suddenly occurred to me then—and I stood up and wandered aimlessly about, overwhelmed by inexplicable thoughts and feeling a dull pressure in my head and heart, that I might have to cry.

And sometimes, when I walked in the evening through the dusty main avenue, filled with the fragrance of blossoming lindens, and saw whispering couples standing in the shadows of the trees; when I saw how two people huddled closely together, as though they could be one person; when I slowly walked there by the softly splashing fountain in the moonlight—then a hot shiver of foreboding ran over me, then the sick Maria entered my mind, then a quiet longing fell upon me for some inexplicable thing and I suddenly saw myself arm in arm with her, strolling down the street in the shadows of the fragrant lindens. And a strange glimmer illuminated Maria's large dark eyes and the moon made her gaunt face look even more pale and transparent. Then I flew upstairs into my attic room. I leant out the window. I looked up into the deep dark sky in which the stars appeared to go out and for hours dwelt on crazed, unsettling dreams until sleep overtook me.

And yet—and yet I have not exchanged ten words with the sick Maria. She never talks. I have only sat by her side for hours at a time and looked into her sick, sad face and always felt over and over again that she would have to die.

In the garden I laid in the grass and inhaled the scent of a thousand flowers; my eyes were intoxicated by the bright colours of the petals, above which the sunlight streamed down, and I listened to the stillness in the air, only interrupted every once in a while by the mating call of a bird. I listened to the fermentation of the moist, fertile earth, this mysterious sound of life ever producing. That time I felt darkly the greatness and beauty of life. That time too was like hearing my life. But then my gaze fell upon the bay window of the house. There I saw the sick Maria sitting—silent and unmoving, with closed eyes. And all my contemplations were once more drawn by the suffering of this one creature, remaining there—turning into a painful but fearfully acknowledged desire that left me puzzled and confused. And fearfully I left the garden, for I had no right to stay in this temple.

So often did I pass by the fence, snapping off, as though in thought, one of the big, bright red, heavily scented roses. Surreptitiously I wanted to then sneak by the window when I saw the trembling, delicate shadow of Maria's figure standing out on the gravel path. And my shadow touched hers as though in an embrace. Then I made for the window as though seized by a fleeting thought and placed the rose, which I had only just broken, in Maria's lap. Then I crept away silently as though I were afraid of being caught.

How many times has this small but seemingly momentous procedure been repeated! I don't know. It is as though I had for the sick Maria laid a thousand roses in her lap, as if our shadows had embraced countless times. Never did Maria mention this episode; but from the glimmer of her big bright eyes I felt that it made her happy.

Perhaps these hours were, as the two of us sat together and silently enjoyed a great, quiet and deep happiness so beautiful that I need not want any more that beautiful. My old uncle let us do so in silence. But one day, as I sat with him in the garden, in the middle of all those bright flowers, with these huge, dreamy yellow butterflies floating above, he said to me in a soft, thoughtful voice: 'Your soul is attracted to suffering, my young man.' And with that he laid his hand upon my head and seemed to want to say something. But he kept quiet. Perhaps he didn't know what he had awakened in me and what has since so forcefully come to life in me.

One day, as I walked up to the window once more at which Maria usually sat, I saw that her face was white and fixed in death. Sunbeams played over her light, delicate form; her loose gold hair fluttered in the wind. It was as if no sickness had consumed her, as though there were no visible cause—an enigma. I placed her last rose in her hand. She took it to the grave.

Soon after Maria's death I departed for a large city. But the memory of those silent days full of sunshine is still alive in me, more vividly than the ear-splitting present. That small town in the valley I will never see again—indeed, I am afraid to look for it again. I don't think I could, even when a strong desire for those eternally young things of the past overwhelm me. For I know I would only search in vain for what is gone without a trace; I would no longer find it there, what still lives in my memory—like today— and it would perhaps just be for me an unnecessary ordeal.

Barabbas

A Fantasy

And it came to pass at the same hour, as they led the Son of Man to Golgotha, that place where robbers and murderers are put to death.

It came to pass at the same high and blazing hour, when his work was done.

It came to pass that at the same hour a noisy mob of people marched through the streets of Jerusalem—and in the midst of these people strode Barabbas, the murderer, and he carried his head defiantly erect.

And around him were bangled harlots with red-painted lips and made-up faces and they hastened after him. And around him were men whose eyes looked drunk on wine and vice. In all their talk lurked the sins of their flesh, and the lewdness of their gestures was the expression of their feelings.

Many who encountered this drunken procession joined with it and called out, 'Barabbas lives!' And all cried, 'Barabbas lives!' Someone shouted 'Hosanna!' as well. But they beat him—for only a few days ago they had cried out 'Hosanna!' to the One who had come parading into the city as a king, and had scattered fresh palm branches in his way. Today, however, they tossed red roses and cheered, 'Barabbas!'

And then they came by a palace, from which they heard harp music and laughter and the noise of a great banquet. And from the house stepped a young man in rich, festive garb. And his hair shined of fragrant oils and his body was scented with the most precious of Arabian perfumes. His eyes were lit up by the joy of the banquet and the smile on his mouth was hot from kissing his concubine.

When the young man recognized Barabbas, he came up to him and spoke thusly. 'Come into my house, O Barabbas, and rest on my softest cushions; come inside, O Barabbas, and my servant girls will rub your body down with the most precious oil of nard. At your feet a girl shall play the lute's sweetest melodies, and from my most precious cup I wish to serve you my fieriest wine. And in that wine I will toss my most precious pearls. O Barabbas, be my guest today—and on this day my guest deserves my concubine, she who is more beautiful than the red dawn in spring. Enter, Barabbas, and crown your head with roses, enjoy this day, for the other one dies on whose head they planted thorns.'

And when the young man spoke thusly, the people cheered him on and Barabbas ascended the marble steps like a champion. And the young man took the roses that crowned his head and placed them around the temples of the murderer Barabbas.

Then he entered the house with him while people cheered in the streets.

Barabbas rested on soft cushions; serving maids rubbed his body down with the most precious oil of nard, and at his feet a girl played the sweetest string music and in his lap sat the youth's concubine who was more beautiful than the red dawn in spring. And there was laughter—and the guests indulged themselves in unheard joys, all of them the Chosen One's enemies and detractors—Pharisees and servants of the priests.

At the hour of one, the young man commanded silence, and all noise ceased.

Then the young man filled his golden cup with the most luscious wine, and in that vessel the wine became like fiery blood. He tossed in a pearl and handed the cup to Barabbas. And the young man reached for a cup made of crystal and toasted Barabbas, 'The Nazarene is dead! Barabbas lives!'

And everyone in the hall cheered, 'The Nazarene is dead! Barabbas lives!'

And the people in the street cried, 'The Nazarene is dead! Barabbas lives!'

But suddenly the sun went out, the earth shook to its foundations and a monstrous horror entered the world. And Creation trembled.

At the same hour the work of redemption was done!

From *A Golden Chalice*

Mary Magdalene

A Dialogue

Outside the gates of the city of Jerusalem. It is evening.

AGATHON. It's time to go back inside the city. The sun is setting and it's already getting dark across the city. It's becoming very still.—But why won't you answer me, Marcellus? Why are you staring away into the distance like that?

MARCELLUS. I've been thinking that in the distance the sea laps at the shores of this country. I've been thinking that beyond the sea that eternal, divine Rome rises to the stars, where no day passes without a celebration. And I'm here on foreign soil. I've been thinking about it all. But I forgot. It's probably time for you to return to the city. It's getting dark. And when it's twilight, a girl waits outside the city gates for Agathon. Don't let her wait, Agathon, don't let her wait, your lady friend. I tell you the women of this country are very strange. I know. They are full of mystery. Don't let her wait, your lady, for you never know what can happen. Terrible things can happen in a minute. You should never lose a minute.

AGATHON. Why are you talking to me like this?

MARCELLUS. I think, since she is pretty, your lady, that you shouldn't make her wait. I tell you, a beautiful woman is something forever inexplicable. The beauty of woman is a mystery. Don't try to understand it. You never know what a beautiful woman can be, what she is forced to do. That's it, Agathon! Oh my—did I know one. Did I know one. I saw things happen which I will never fathom. No man would ever fathom them. We never get to the bottom of what happens.

AGATHON. What did you see happen? I beg you, tell me more!

MARCELLUS. Let's go. Perhaps the hour's come when I can tell you without having to shudder at my own words and thoughts.

They walk slowly, going back on the road to Jerusalem. Stillness surrounds them.

MARCELLUS. It happened on a sweltering summer night, when this fever lingers in the air and the moon clouds one's wits. Then I saw her. It was in a small tavern. She danced there bare-footed on a costly rug. Never have I seen a woman dance more beautiful, never more intoxicated. The rhythm of her body gave me strange dark visions that sent a hot, feverish shiver shaking through my body. To me it was as though this woman were playing with unseen, secret, delightful things in her dance, as though she were embracing some godlike being that one never saw, as though she were kissing red lips that bowed longingly to hers. Her motions were of the most sublime pleasure. As though she were being covered with caresses. As though she were seeing things that we could not, and performing with them in her dance. She enjoyed the incredible ecstasy of her body. Perhaps she lifted her mouth to sweet, delicious fruit and sipped fiery wine when she threw her head back and directed her eyes longingly upward. No! I understood nothing, and yet everything was strangely alive—it was there. And then she dropped to our feet, naked, only her hair spilling over her. As if the night had been balled up into a black knot in her hair and carried her away from us. And she gave herself away, gave away her glorious body, gave it to anyone who wanted it. I saw her make love with beggars and common men, saw her with princes and kings. She was some glorious hetaera. Her body, a precious vessel of joy. I saw this world never more beautiful. Her life belonged only to joy. I saw her dance at feasts and her body was showered by roses. Yet she stood amid the brightest of them like one newly bloomed, the sole beautiful flower. And I saw her crown the statue of Dionysus with flowers, saw her embrace the cold marble as though she were embracing her lover. She choked on her burning, feverish kisses.—And then someone came, who walked past, wordless, without gesture, clad in a hair shirt, dust on his feet. This man walked past and regarded her—and was gone. But she looked at Him, unable to move—and walked, walked, and followed this strange prophet who had maybe beckoned to her with his eyes, followed His call and dropped to His feet. She humbled herself before Him—and looked upon Him as though upon a god. She served Him the same way the men served Him, who were to either side of Him.

AGATHON. You still haven't come to the end. I feel you've still something to say.

MARCELLUS. I don't know any more. No! But one day I learnt that they wanted to nail that strange prophet to a cross. I learnt this from our governor Pilate. And seeing as I wanted to go up to Golgotha, wanted to see Him, wanted to see Him die. Maybe some mysterious occurrence would appear to me. I wanted to look into His eyes. Maybe His eyes would have spoken to me. I believe they would have spoken.

AGATHON. And you didn't go!

MARCELLUS. I was on the way up there. But I turned around. Because I felt that I would meet someone up there, on her knees before the cross, praying to him, listening to the fleeing of His life. In rapture. And so I turned around once more. And inside of me it remained dark.

AGATHON. But what of that other queer fellow?—No, we don't want to speak about that!

MARCELLUS. Let's say nothing of it, Agathon! We can do nothing but.—Just look, Agathon, how it smoulders strange and dark in the clouds. You would think that beyond them burns an ocean of flames. A divine fire! And the sky—like a blue bell. As if one could hear it ring in deep, solemn tones. One might even think that up there in those unreachable heights something goes on of which you will never know a thing. But there are times when one might have some inkling, when a great silence is descending upon the earth. And yet! All this is very confusing. The gods love to leave unsolvable riddles for us humans. But the earth doesn't save us from the cunning of the gods, for it too is full of this seduction of the senses. These things confuse me and people. Of course! These things are kept very quiet! And the human soul doesn't reveal its mystery. When one asks, it remains silent.

AGATHON. We want to live and not ask. Life is full of beauty.

MARCELLUS. We'll never know much. Indeed! And that's why it's better to forget that which we know. Enough of this! We are almost there. Just look how deserted the streets are. No more people to see. (*A wind rises.*) That is a voice, one telling us to look up at the stars. And be silent.

AGATHON. Marcellus, look how high the grain grows in the fields. Each ear bends to the earth—heavy with grain. There are going to be days of a glorious harvest.

MARCELLUS. Yes! Festive days! Festive days, my Agathon!

AGATHON. I'm going to walk with Rachel through the fields, through this fruitful, blessed land. O you glorious life!

MARCELLUS. You're right! Enjoy your youth. Mere youth is beauty! It befits me to wander in the dark. And here we part ways. With yours a mistress awaits—with mine the silence of the night! Live well, Agathon! It's going to be a beautiful night. You can stay outside a long time.

AGATHON. And you can look up at the stars—at this enormous serenity. I want to go joyfully on my way and praise the beauty. That way you honour yourself and the gods.

MARCELLUS. Do as you say, and you'll do right! Farewell, Agathon!

AGATHON (*thoughtfully*). I want to ask you one more thing. Don't think anything of it when I ask. What was the name of that strange prophet? Tell me!

MARCELLUS. What good would it do you to know! I forgot his name. But no! I remember. I remember. He was called Jesus and was from Nazareth!

AGATHON. I thank you! Fare you well! May the gods be well disposed towards you, Marcellus! (*He goes.*)

MARCELLUS (*lost in thought*). Jesus!—Jesus! And he was from Nazareth. (*He goes slowly and thoughtfully on his way. It has turned night and countless stars light the sky.*)

Neglect

1

Nothing disturbs the silence of neglect any more. Above the dark, age-old treetops, the clouds pass over and are mirrored in the green-blue water of the lake seemingly bottomless. And motionless, as though rapt in sombre submission, lies the surface—day in, day out.

In the middle of this silent lake, the castle rises towards the clouds with peaked, battered towers and rooftops. The black, broken walls are rank with weeds, and the sunlight is reflected off the round, blind windows. In the dim, dark courtyards, pigeons fly about and search for hiding places amid the cracks in the masonry.

They seem to always be afraid of something, for they fly in panic and haste by the windows. Below in the court-yard, the fountain splashes quiet and subdued. From the fountain's bronze basin, the thirsty pigeons drink now and then.

Through the narrow, dusty paths of the castle, a dull, feverish breeze sometimes prowls, which terrifies the bats into fluttering upwards. Otherwise nothing disturbs this deep repose.

But the apartments are black with dust! High and bare and freezing and full of perished objects. Once in a while, through the blind windows, comes a tiny light that the darkness once more absorbs. Here, the past has died.

One day it congealed into a single, twisted rose here. In its lifelessness, the time passes without regard.

And the silence of neglect pierced everything.

2

No one can trespass the park any more. The branches of the trees entwine themselves a thousandfold. The entire park is but one single, gigantic living thing.

And an eternal night sleeps beneath the enormous canopy of leaves. And deep silence! And the air is saturated with the pall of rot!

But sometimes the park wakes from its ponderous dreams. Then it streams with a memory from cold starry nights, of deeply hidden secret places, when it listened to the feverish kisses and embraces, of summer nights full of shining splendour and glory, when the moon magically cast wild images upon the black ground, of people who strolled along gracefully, gallantly full of rhythmic motion beneath its leafy canopy, who whispered sweet, mad words with fine, auspicious smiles.

And then once more the park sinks back into its death sleep.

Shadows roll on the water with copper beeches and pines, and from the depths of the pond comes a dead, sad murmur.

Swans meander through the glimmering waters, slowly, unmoving, their slender necks rigidly held upwards. They snake on! Around the dying castle! Day in! Day out!

White lilies grow at the edges of the lake amid the blinding-coloured grass. And their shadows in the water are whiter than they are themselves.

And if some die away, others come out of the depths. And they are like small, dead hands of women.

Large fish swim curious around the pale flowers with glassy, staring eyes and then submerge once more into the depths—noiselessly!

And the silence of neglect pierced everything.

3

And sitting above in a fissured tower room sits the count. Day in, day out. He follows the clouds that pass over the treetops, illuminated and pure. He enjoys watching the sun shining in the clouds during the evening, as it sets. He is keen to the sounds on high: to the cries of birds that fly by the tower or to the roaring echo of the wind when it sweeps about the castle.

He watches while the park sleeps, dull and heavy, and sees the swans meander through the glittering waters—that wash around the castle. Day in! Day out!

And the water shimmers green-blue. But in the water the clouds mirror themselves as they pass over the castle; and in the waters their shadows light beaming and pure, as they do themselves. The water lilies wave to him like the small, dead hands of women, and bob along after the quiet sounds of the wind, dreamily sad.

And the poor count beholds what is all dying around him, like a little, lost child over whom hangs a fate which has no more strength to go on, which is fading away like a shadow before noon.

He no longer hears the little, tragic melody of his soul: the past!

When evening comes, he lights his old soot-black lamp and reads from voluminous, yellowed books of the past great and glorious.

He reads with a feverish, pounding heart until the present, to which he does not belong, subsides. And the shadows of the past rise up—giant. And he lives that life, that gloriously beautiful life of his forefathers.

At night, when the storm scuds around the tower, such that walls groan to their foundation and the frightened birds scream outside his window, a nameless sadness overcomes the count.

Upon his tired, centuries-old soul weighs his fate.

And he presses his face against the window and peers into the night outside. And then everything seems gigantically dreamlike, spectral! And terrible. Through the castle he listens to the storm rage, as though it wanted to sweep away everything dead and scatter it to the wind.

But when the tortured figment of the night drops away like a shade summoned forth—once more the silence of neglect pierced everything.

The Morning Song

Come down now, boy Titan,
And wake her the much-loved sleeper!
Come down and bind
That dreaming head with tender blossoms.
Set fire to the worried sky with a burning brand,
So that the blanching stars resound dancing
And the flying veils of the night
Go up in flames,
So that the cyclopean clouds disperse,
In which the winter, fleeing the earth,
Still threatens howling with icy shivers,
And the heavenly distances part in luminous purity.
And step then, you glorious being with flying locks,
Upon the earth, the proud suitor she accepts
With blissful silence, and trembling with deep shivers
From your so wild, storm-mad embrace,
She opens her holy womb to you.
And to herself this inebriate has the sweetest premonition,
As you a maker of glowing flowers awaken
The budding life within her, of this exalted past
Urged towards a higher future,
Which resembles you as you resemble yourself,

And yielding to your will, ever quicker,
So that in her an eternal enigma
Is henceforth and once more renewed in exalted beauty.

Dreamwalker

Where are you, she who walked by my side,
Where are you, heaven's face?
A rude wind in my ear teases me: You fool!
A dream! A dream! You clown!
But still, but still! Was it not like that once,
Before I walked in night and desolation?
You know it very well, you fool, you clown!
My soul's echo, this rude wind:
O fool! O clown!
She stood with imploring hands,
With a tragic smile on her lips,
And called in night and desolation!
She called one thing! You don't remember?
What love sounds like. No echo came
Back to her, to her this word.
Was it love? Woe, so that's what I forgot!
Just night and desolation surround me,
And my soul's echo—the wind!
Which teases and teases: O fool! O clown!

The Three Ponds in Hellbrunn

'The First'

Around the flowers bottle flies spin,
Around pale flowers on a dead flood,
Be gone! Be gone! The air, it burns!
In the depths glow the coals of decay!
The willow weeps, the silent one stares,
A sticky pall brews on the water.
Be gone! Be gone! This is the place
For the loathsome couplings of black toads.

'The Second'

Scenes of clouds, flowers and people—
Sing out, sing out, exultant world!
A smiling innocence mirrors you—
Heaven is everything which pleases her—
She graciously changes darkness into light.
The far becomes near. O you happy man!
Sun, clouds, flowers and people
Breathe this godly tranquillity in bliss.

'The Third'

The waters shimmer greenish blue
And the cypresses breathe calmly,
The evening sounds deep as a bell—
Here the depth grows immeasurable.
The moon rises, the night turns blue,
Blossoms in the waters' reflection—
An enigmatic sphinx's face,
Thereon my heart wishes to bleed out.

St Peter's Cemetery

Rock solitude rings everything.
Death's pale flowers are shivering
On the graves, which grieve in the darkness—
Yet this grief lacks any sorrow.

Heaven smiles silently downwards
Into this dream-cloistered garden,
Where its quiet pilgrims await.
The cross watches on every grave.

The church rises up like a prayer
Before a scene of eternal mercy,
Under columned walks many lights burn,
Which mutely beseech for poor souls—

While the trees blossom in the night,
Such that death's face is shrouded over
In the shimmering store of its beauty,
Which makes the dead dream the deeper.

Collation of 1909

I think it must be awful to live this way forever, fully conscious of every animal drive, which spins life through time. I felt, smelt and touched the most fearful possibilities in me and heard demons howling in my blood, which a thousand devils with their pricks drive the flesh mad. What a terrible nightmare!

Georg Trakl to his older sister, Mina von Rauterberg,
October 1908

In the late summer of 1908, Trakl left the White Angel and Salzburg to continue his pharmaceutical studies at the University of Vienna. He had only published sporadically in newspapers after 1906, and seemed less the serious writer now and more the '*Spinner*'—a screwball, a harmless eccentric. His sister Grete, however, saw him as a special person, a true poet. Although she had often been away at boarding school, Georg had corresponded with her and each became the other's confidante. Thus, through their letters and brief contacts during her holidays, the rapport and intense bond between the two siblings increased as did perhaps that tendency for the younger one to emulate the older.

Since their parents had higher hopes for Grete, Georg may have had to moderate his influence on her and meet her interest and enthusiasm for him with a degree of caution and even distance. Considered himself a dangerous character, a kind of Raskolnikov, he had to be careful what he said to Grete and how he rubbed off on her—not only for their parents' peace of mind but also for hers. But he did not want to warn her away either—he wanted to share himself with her, and, like his drugs, played with the dosage of his contact with her, his good effect and what he wanted her to know about his feelings. This came across in the books she should read—which were the books he read and identified with. One of these was certainly a birthday present for her as well as a telling parting gift before he left for university— a copy of Flaubert's *Madame Bovary*. The novel itself was a risqué present, one in which Grete might see her brother in the character of the 'health officer' Charles Bovary—but what about herself? Was she not unlike his youthful and ultimately unfaithful young wife Emma? Georg's inscription is even more telling and erotic, hinting that one has corrupted the other: 'For my beloved little demon,' he writes, 'who has risen from the sweetest and deepest tale of 1001 Nights. in memorium.'

What tales does he mean?

What should be remembered?

Scheherazade tells stories within stories and finds their 'depth' in that way. The word Trakl uses also points directly to a story of interment as incest. In 'The First Kalandar's Tale', two male friends, cousins, get drunk on wine. One extracts a promise of silence from the other and then leaves and returns with a richly adorned and veiled young woman. The three embark to a cemetery, where a tomb has been broken open, exhumed and made into a richly appointed subterranean vault shielded by an iron door. As the one cousin and his female companion descend, he asks the other to close the iron door behind him. Later, the cousin aboveground suffers a misadventure in which he is forced to tell the secret of the buried couple to the grand vizier, their father. On hearing their fate, he, too, has a secret to tell:

> O son of my brother, this youth from his boyhood was
> madly in love with his sister and often I forbade him

from her, saying to myself, 'They are but little ones.' However, when they grew up, sin befell between them, and although I could hardly believe it, I confined him and chided him and threatened him with the severest threats, and the eunuchs and servants said to him: 'Beware of so foul a thing which none before thee ever did' . . . . After that I lodged them apart and shut her up, but the accursed girl loved him with passionate love, for Satan had got the mastery of her as well as of him and made their foul sin seem fair in their sight.

The subterranean love nest is exposed and in it is found the corpses of the lovers burnt almost beyond recognition by God's wrath.

For Georg, life in the imperial capital during the 'Vienna Renaissance' and the Austrian Secession proved both overstimulating and overwhelming. Although friends had invited him to visit, he had never accepted their offers nor really lived anywhere else but in Salzburg. He wrote to his sister Maria Geipel about how much he hated Vienna and the Viennese themselves—a 'stupid lot' who, behind their 'unpleasant Bonhomie', hid their 'fatuous and vulgar qualities'. In time, however, one of those friends, Erhard Buschbeck, helped him find his proper milieu among the young writers and artists of the 'Academic Society for Literature and Music'. Buschbeck even interceded in having some of Trakl's poems published in journals such as *Merkur* (*Mercury*) and *Ton und Wort* (*Sound and Word*). The writer Hermann Bahr, a leading member of the Young Vienna group of the 1890s, became an early admirer of Trakl's verse, seeing him as a new and Austrian Rimbaud, and chose three poems for publication in yet another of Vienna's literary journals.

Trakl's reputation grew despite the reserve he displayed in Vienna's cafes and coffeehouses, and he was befriended by composer Arnold Schoenberg, social and literary critic Karl Kraus, writer Peter Altenberg, architect Adolf Loos and his actress wife Bessie, and Loos' protégé, painter Oskar Kokoschka.

How close he felt to some of these individuals is apparent in the poems he dedicated to them. And despite the praise and publication that he enjoyed during the Vienna period, from 1908 to 1910, he was disappointed in his work and considered the poems which comprise the 'Collation of 1909' as meritless. Though revealing his debt to the French Symbolists, they anticipate the work to come as well as the incredible melancholy and loneliness that he suffered—even after he came to accept his new life in Vienna, his new friends and the comforts of chain-smoking, alcohol and drugs. These poems recorded a certain passion and eroticism which counterpoint the overarching despair.

Meanwhile, Grete had graduated from her boarding school outside Vienna and rented an apartment in the city proper during the autumn of 1909, so as to be close to the music academy where she trained as a concert pianist. Her presence in her brother's life can be detected in his correspondence with friends, in which Trakl describes that something momentous has raised his spirits and provided him with a happiness that he did not have before.

As much as he might enjoy the unsupervised companionship of his sister, they were hardly the dyad, the couple which could be read into the poems.. Grete, the 'inexperienced girl' fresh from finishing school, fell in love with Trakl's best friend, Erhard Buschbeck. Trakl's role in their relationship is unknown, but he surely approved and it made it possible for him to maintain some distance from her, not only for appearance sake but for maintaining a natural and purely mental relationship between siblings who would otherwise not need anyone else (as Robert Musil imagined between Ulrich and Agathe in The Man without Qualities). Unfortunately, Grete had to compete with the prostitutes whom Buschbeck saw on a weekly basis—and he did not reciprocate her advances beyond anything but the same friendship he showed her brother. Thus, Grete's time in Vienna during the cold winter of 1909–10 was marked by depression, disappointment and loneliness which she treated in the same way that her brother treated his—with opium. She even asked Buschbeck to procure the drug for her.

Those who see an incestuous relationship between Georg and Grete, or the continuation of one, as the result of some incident of sexual abuse in childhood, point to this time in Vienna. However, from what little evidence there is, one can also see little contact between the two, distance rather than salacious and forbidden assignations behind the closed doors of her rented room or his. Their doors are still as impenetrable as the iron door in the story from *1001 Nights*. And Georg's friends, well acquainted with, seasoned in and sentient to a good scandal, only saw the natural affection between brother and sister. Indeed, the brother and sister Trakl appeared in public as innocent as any pair, whether siblings or cousins. There is some evidence of this and one can only read so far with it. When the weather warmed in April, following an early March Easter, Grete and Georg strolled through the amusement park in Vienna's Prater and posed for the silhouette artist who scissored a young woman in her Sunday best and a smart straw hat and a young man sporting a cravat.

Where the iron door opens is only in the poems.

Three Dreams

1

It seems that I dreamt of leaves falling,
Of distant forests and of dark seas,
Of sad words echoing on and on—
Yet I could catch none of their meaning.

It seems that I dreamt of stars falling,
Of pale eyes weeping in entreaty,
Of a smile echoing on and on—
Yet I could catch none of its meaning.

Like leaves falling, like stars falling,
I saw myself ever coming and going,
A dream's undying echo going on and on—
Yet I could catch none of its meaning.

2

In the dark mirror which is my soul
Are pictures of a sea never seen,
Of forsaken lands tragic and fantastic,
Melting into blueness, inexactness.

My soul gave birth to a sky of blood crimson,
Penetrated by gigantic, raining suns,

And shimmering gardens strangely come to life,
Seething of sensuous and deadly pleasures.

And the dark wellspring which is my soul
Produced images of monstrous nights,
Set into motion by nameless songs
And the breathings of eternal powers.

My soul shakes from memory's darkness,
As though it found itself in everything—
In unfathomable seas and nights
And in deep songs with no beginning or end.

3

I saw many cities flame ravished
And the era pile horror on horror,
And I saw many people turn to dust,
And everything slip into oblivion.

I saw the gods plunge into the night,
The most sacred harps smashed to pieces powerless,
And out of decay kindles anew,
A new life emerging at daylight.

Emerging at daylight and gone once more,
The eternally same tragedy,
Which we play without comprehending,

And whose maddening nighted torment
Crowns the beauty's soft Gloria
As a smiling universe of thorns.

Of Still Days

So ghostlike are these late days coming to be,
The same way the look of the sick is, sent here
Into the light. But the night to which they turned
Already shadows the mute plaint of their eyes.

It seems that they smile and think about their feasts,
The way one trembles for songs half-forgotten
And tries to find the words for a sad gesture,
Which fades into immeasurable silence.

Thus does the sun still play around sick flowers
And allows out of a deathly cool pleasure
For them to shiver in the wispy, clear breeze.

The red forests whisper and fade in twilight,
And deathlier night stops the woodpeckers' hammer,
The same way an echo does from musty tombs.

Twilight

You are dishevelled, wracked by every pain
And shake from every jarring melody,
You a broken harp—a wretched heart,
From which blossom misery's sick flowers.

Who bid your adversary, your killer,
The one who stole the last spark of your soul,
The way he degodded this barren world
Into a whore foul, sick, pale with decay!

From the shadows a wild dance takes the floor,
To a tangled, tattered, soulless tune,
A reel, which circles beauty's crown of thorns,

Which limply crowns the victor, the one lost,
—A terrible prize wrested for despair,
And which doesn't appease the bright godhead.

The Horror

I saw myself walking through abandoned rooms.
—The stars spun madly upon a blue background,
And the dogs bayed loudly out in the fields,
And the foehn wind tossed wild in the treetops.

But suddenly: Stillness! A dull fever
Makes poisonous flowers bloom from my mouth,
From the branches drips a pale shimmering dew
As though from a wound, drips and drips like blood.

From a mirror's deceptively empty void
Slowly rises, as though in a vague likeness
Out of horror and from blackness: Cain!

Very softly rustle the doorway's velvet drapes,
Through the window the moon too peers at nothing,
Then am I alone with my murderer.

Devotion

That unforsakenness of my younger years
Is a silent devotion at tolling bells,
At the darkening altar of every church
And the heavenly expanse of their blue domes.

At an evening melody on an organ,
At broad squares of fading away with the dark,
And at a fountain's splashing, soft and gentle
And sweet, like the silly patter of children.

I see myself dreaming hushed with hands folded,
And whispering prayers forgotten long ago,
And my look benighted by despair too soon.

Then there shimmers from out of entangled shapes
A female figure, shrouded in dark mourning,
And pours in me the chalice of wicked chills.

Sabbath

A blast of fevered, noxious vegetation
Causes me to dream during lunar twilights,
And I feel myself gently entwined, embraced
And see what looks like a mad witches' sabbath

Blood-coloured blooms in the brightness of mirrors
Pressing flaming animal lusts from my heart
And their lips, which are practised in every art,
Swelling furiously on my drunken gorge.

Pestilential-hued flowers of tropic shores,
Which administer to my lips their goblets,
The turbid wells of slaver for vile tortures.
And one of them swallows—O frenzied maenad—

My flesh, made weary by the fumes of such heat
And pain-raptured by fearsome animal lusts.

Hymn to the Night

1

Born out of the shadow of a breath,
We wander in forsakenness
And are forlorn in eternity,
Like victims unknowing why they were offered.

As beggars nothing belongs to us,
We fools before the shuttered gate.
Like the blind we heed to the silence,
Where our speaking in whispers went lost.

We are the wanderers with no end,
The clouds, which the wind scatters away,
The flowers shivering in death's cold,
Waiting until someone mows them down.

2

So that the last agony leaves me fulfilled,
I won't fight you, your hostile and dark forces.
You are the street down into the vast silence,
Upon which we walk in the coldest nights.

Your breathing makes me burn even more loudly,
Be patient! The star gutters out, the dreams float
In those realms which never give their names to us,
And which we can only dare pursue dreamless.

3

You dark night, you dark heart,
Who mirrors your holiest depths
And the final gulfs of your malice?
The mask gazes before our pain—

Before our pain, before our lust
The stone laughter of the empty mask,
Thereon these earthen things were broken
And we ourselves without knowing.

And a strange foe stands before us,
Who mocks, for whom we struggle dying,
Such that our songs sound ever bleaker
And what weeps in us remains dark.

4

You are the wine which makes one drunk,
Now I shed my blood in sweet dances
And must wreathe my sorrow with flowers!
Thus your deepest desire, O night!

I am the harp in your bosom,
Now for the last of my sufferings
Your dark song wrestles inside my heart
And makes me immortal, irreal.

5

Deep quiet—O deep quiet!
Not one pious bell is ringing,
You sweet mother of suffering—
Your peace is spreading deathly wide.

With your cool, beneficent
Hands, close every single wound—
Such that they shed blood from within—
Sweet mother of suffering—you!

6

O let my silence be your song!
What shall the pauper whisper you,
He who left the gardens of life?
Let you be nameless within me—

Who grew within me dreamlessly,
Like a bell that made not a sound,
Like the sweet bride of my sufferings
And the drunk poppies of my sleep.

7

I hear flowers die in the ground
And the fountains' drunken lament
And a song from a bell's mouth,
The night, and a whispered question;
And a heart—O mortally wounded,
Going beyond its impoverished days.

8

The darkness blots out my silence,
I was a dead shadow in the day—
Then I stepped from the house of joy
Out in the night.

Now a silence lives within my heart,
Which does not feel after a barren day—
And like thorns laughing softly at you,
Night—on and on!

9

O night, you the mute gate before my song,
Behold this dark stigmata shedding blood
And the trembling cup of pain fully tipped!
O night, I am ready!

O night, you garden of oblivion
Around my poverty's world-cloistered blaze,

The wine leaves wither, the crown of thorns wilts.
O come, you high time!

10

In the past my demon would laugh,
When I was a light in shimmering gardens
And had sport and dance for my companions
And the wine of love which made me drunk.

In the past my demon would weep,
When I was a light in gardens full of pain
And had humility for my companion,
Whose blaze lights this poverty's house.

Now my demon does not weep but laughs,
I am a shadow of those lonely gardens
And have for my death-dark companion
The silence of the empty midnight.

11

My meagre smile, which struggled for you,
My sobbing song fading into the dark.
Now will my path come to an end.

Let me enter your cathedral
As before, a fool, plain, pious,
And facing you in silent prayer.

12

You exist within deep midnight,
A dead shore along a sea of silence,
A dead shore: no longer any more!
You exist within deep midnight.

You exist within deep midnight,
The sky in which you glowed like a star,
A sky from which God thrives no longer.
You exist within deep midnight.

You exist within deep midnight
One unbegotten in a sweet womb,
And never having been, irreal!
You exist within deep midnight.

The Deep Song

I have been released from deep night.
My soul marvels in immortality,
My soul's listening across space and time
To eternity's melody!
Day nor delight, night nor sorrow
Is eternity's melody,
And ever since I heard eternity,
I nevermore feel lust and woe!

Ballad

A fool inscribed three signs in the sand,
A pale maidservant stood before him.
Loud sang, O sang the sea.

There she held a beaker in her hand,
That shimmered all the way to the brim,
Like blood so red and thick.

Not one word was spoken—the sun waned,
Whereupon the fool took the beaker
From her hand and drank it dry.

Then its light extinguished in her hand,
The wind scattered three signs in the sand—
Loud sang, O sang the sea.

Ballad

There laments a heart: You can't find her,
Her home is probably far from here,
And her face is unfamiliar!
It is night weeping at a door!

In the Marble Hall burns light after light,
O gloom, O gloom! Who's dying here!
Somewhere whispers: O you're not coming?
It is night weeping at a door!

A sobbing still: O he saw the light!
Then it became dark here and there—
A sobbing: Brother, O you're not praying?
It is night weeping at a door.

Ballad

A sweltering garden is the night.
We kept it secret, which seized us terribly.
From then on our hearts awakened
And sank under the weight of silence.

No star would blossom in this night.
And there was no one who asked for us.
Only a demon laughed in the darkness.
You're all damned! With that the deed was done.

Melusine

The night weeps against my window—
The night is mute, it must be the wind that weeps,
The wind, the way a lost child would—
What is it that makes it weep so?
O poor Melusine!

Like fire her hair blows in the storm,
Like fire in passing clouds and she moans—
For in your favour, you poor maid,
My heart says a silent night prayer.
O poor Melusine!

Downfall

A wind is blowing! The green candles
Sing being put out—huge and full
The moon suffuses the great hall,
Through which parties no longer resound.

Ancestral portraits smile quietly
And far—their final shadow fell,
The room is stifling with decay,
In which the ravens mutely circle.

A lonely feeling of bygone times
Is staring from out of stone masks,
Twisted in pain and void of life,
Mourning away in desolation.

The sickly smells of drowning gardens
Flirt softly around the downfall—
Like an echo of words being sobbed,
Wavering above the vacant tombs.

Poem

A pious song occurred to me:
You humble heart, you sacred blood,
O snatch me from such wicked fire!
Thus was it heard and pleas no more!

My heart's heavy with every sin
And consumed in a wicked fire,
And calls not on the sacred blood
And is so mute and void of tears.

Night Song

Across the dark floods of the night,
I sing my songs full of sadness,
Songs, ones which are bleeding from wounds,
But no heart brings them here for me
Again through the dark.

Only the dark floods of the night
Are rushing, sobbing with songs,
Songs, ones which are bleeding from wounds,
Which bring them back here to my heart
Again through the dark.

At a Window

The sky blue above the rooftops,
And clouds, which are blowing over,
Before the window a tree in the spring dew,

And a bird flicks drunkenly skywards,
A lost fragrance from the blossoms—
A heart can feel: This is the world!

The silence grows and the noon blazes!
My God how the world is so rich!
I dream and dream and this life takes flight,

This life outside of here—far from me
Somewhere through a sea of loneliness!
A heart feels this and finds no joy!

Upon the Death of an Old Woman

Often I listen full of horror at the door
And I enter, thinking that someone fled,
And her eyes see dreamily beyond me,
As though they saw me in some other place.

Thus she sits yielding inside and listens
And seems far from the things which surround her,
But shakes when a noise is at the window,
And then weeps to herself like a scared child,

And with a weary hand strokes her white hair
And asks with a pale look: Must I go now?
And fever wild: That light on the altar,
Put it out! Where are you going? What happened?

Gypsies

The longing slowly cools in their nighted eyes
Searching for that homeland they can never find.
So in this way an ill fate drives them onwards,
One only melancholy might wholly plumb.

The clouds wander out ahead of their travels,
And sometimes a flock of birds might escort them,
Until evening when they lose sight of their trail,
And sometimes the wind carries an Ave's bells

Into the stellar solitude of their camp,
Such that their songs swell filling with yearning
And sob of their ancestral curse and affliction,
On which no stars of hope softly shine their light.

Outdoor Theatre

Now I step through the slender archway!
Chaotic footsteps in the streets
Scatter and a faint whisper of words
From people as they walk on past.

I am standing before a green stage!
Do it, do it again, you game
Of lost days with no guilt and penance,
Only ghostlike, strange and cold!

To the melody of early days,
I see myself going up there again,
A child, whose faint, forgotten lament
I watch weeping, strange to what I know.

Your astonished face turned towards the evening,
Was I once this, the one who makes me weep now,
Like your gesticulations unending still,
Which point mute and trembling at the night.

To Slacken

A rotting of dream-created paradises
Blows around this mournful, lethargic heart,
Which only drinks disgust from all which is sweet,
And then bleeds itself out in vulgar pain.

Now it pounds to the beat of faded dances,
To the despair of sombre melodies,
While the starry garlands of some ancient hope
Wither on a long degodded altar.

From the delirium of perfumes and wines
Your vigilant feeling of shame remains—
Yesterday in a contorted reflection—
And the everyday world's grey grief smites you.

Coda

From the day departed the last, pale light,
The early passions have died away,
Spilt is the sacred wine of my joys,
Now my heart weeps at night and listens

For the echo of its youthful revels
Losing itself so softly in the dark,
So shadowlike, the way faded leaves fall
On a lonely grave in the autumn night.

Unison

Extremely luminous tones in the thin air,
They are singing this day's faraway grieving,
Which wholly suffused with unimagined scents
Makes us dream for never-felt shivers of awe.

As silent prayers said for lost companions
And quiet echoes of pleasures lost in night,
The leaves fall in the long-abandoned gardens,
Which sun themselves in paradisiac silence.

In the bright mirror of clarified waters
We see this dead time strangely brought back to life
And our passions within the bleeding away,
Lifting up our souls towards more distant heavens.

We undergo this death to be newly made
For these deeper tortures and deeper pleasures,
Therein does the mysterious godhead reign—
And us perfected by eternal new suns.

Crucifixus

He is the god before whom the poor genuflect,
He the mirror of fate of their earthly torments,
A pallid god, violated, spat upon,
Perished on the hill of the murderers' shame.

They kneel before his flesh's need of torture,
So that their meekness is married to him,
And so that the night and death of his last look
Steels their hearts in the ice of longing to die—

So that his death-nighted head bedecked in thorns
—symbol of earthly affliction—will open
The gate to paradises of poverty,
Where the pale angel and the one lost welcome.

Confiteor

The gaily coloured pictures which life paints
I see turn sombre only with the twilight,
Like a skewed, crumpled shadow, bleak and cold,
Those scarcely born already, conquered by death.

And thereupon the mask dropped from each thing,
I see just fear, decay, shame and pestilence,
Humanity's hero-less tragedy,
A terrible play, performed on graves, corpses.

This desolate vision nauseates me,
Yet a despotic order wants that I stay on,
A comedian who delivers his role,
Forced to, full of desolation—tedium!

Silence

Across the forests the moon shines
Pale, which causes us to dream,
The willows by the dark pond
Weep soundless in the night

A heart dies—and softly
The mist floods in and rises—
Silence, silence!

Before Sunrise

In the darkness clamour the many birdsongs,
The trees are rushing loudly and the brooks,
A pink-coloured glimmer resounds in the clouds
Like love's first anguish. The night turns blue—

With shy hands the half-light tenderly smooths out
The bed of love, feverishly tangled,
And lets the rapture of slackened kisses end
In dreams, smiling and feeling half-awake.

Blood Guilt

The night is looming at our bed of kisses.
From somewhere whispers: Who assumes your guilt?
Still shaking from the sweetness of shameful lust,
We pray: Forgive us, Mary, in your mercy!

From bowls of flowers rise yearning fragrances,
Caressing our foreheads ashen with guilt,
Limp amid the breath of the sweltering breeze,
We dream: Forgive us, Mary, in your mercy!

But the fountain of sirens rushes louder
And the sphinx rears up darker at our guilt,
Such that our hearts echo once more full of sin,
We sob: Forgive us, Mary, in your mercy!

Meeting

Strangers en route—we behold ourselves
And when our weary eyes meet they ask:
What have you accomplished with your life?
Be still! Be still! Stop all your wailing!

Around us it is cooler now,
The clouds disperse into the far distance.
I think, we don't ask any longer
And no one will lead us into the night.

Accomplishment

My brother, let us walk softer!
The streets gently fade into darkness.
From afar flags surely glance and flutter.
But brother, let us be alone—

And lie looking into the sky,
Meek and fully willing in heart,
And unmindful of our past conduct.
My brother, look, the world is wide!

Out there the wind plays with the clouds,
Which come as we do, from here or there.
Let us be ourselves, like flowers,
So poor, my brother, so lovely and bright!

Metamorphosis

An eternal light glows dark red,
A heart so red, lacking in sin!
Hailed thou art, O Mary!

Your pale effigy is in bloom
And a shrouded body starts to glow,
O lady thou, Mary!

Your womb burns in sweet agonies,
As your eyes smile hurtful and enormous,
O mother thou, Mary!

Evening Walk

I go walking into the evening,
The wind runs along and sings:
You, one spellbound by every glow,
O feel what wrestles with you!

The voice of a dead woman, whom I loved,
Speaks: Poor is the heart of fools!
Forget, forget that which troubles your soul!
That which becomes is your pain!

The Saint

When, in that hell of self-created afflictions,
Ghastly obscene images oppressed him—
No heart was ever so beguiled as his
By lust without the urge, without the heart
So racked by God—he lifts his worn hands,
The ones unredeemed, in prayer to heaven.
Only an agonizingly unstilled lust
Gives form to his love-fevered prayer, whose fire
Goes sweeping through mystic eternities,
And the *evoë* of Dionysus
Does not sound so drunk as when in deadly,
Foaming-mouthed ecstasy his tortured cry
Wrings fulfilment: *Exaudi me, O Maria*!

To a Woman in Passing

I met a face in passing once
Expressing such absolute pain,
Which seemed strongly and secretly kindred,
As though God sent—
And she walked on past and vanished.

I met a face in passing once
Expressing such absolute pain,
Which left me spellbound,
As though I had recognized someone,
Her I once called beloved in a dream,
In some life, which vanished long ago.

The Dead Church

They sit crowded together on dark pews
And lift their dead expressions to the cross.
The candles shimmer as though they were draped,
And dim and as though draped, the wounded head.
From its golden pot the incense rises
On high, the dying down hymn breathes its last,
And with uncertainty and sweetness this room
Darkens as though haunted. The priest steps
To the altar, but performs the pious rites
With a weary spirit to me—a bad actor
Before the vile bead-tellers with frozen hearts,
In a soulless performance with bread and wine.
The bell rings! The candles flicker dimmer
And paler, as though draped, the wounded head!
The organ swells! In dead hearts there shudders
Up a memory! A bleeding face of pain
Shrouds itself in darkness and that desolation
From many eyes stares after him into the void.
And someone, she who sounds like every voice,
Sobs upwards—as the horror grew in the room,
The horror of death grew: Have mercy on us—
Lord!

Poems, 1909–1912

I would very much like to enshroud myself completely and become invisible somewhere else. And there is always sticking to words or, better said, to this terrifying impotence!

Georg Trakl to Erhard Buschbeck, July 1910

It seems that now I walk around all day like a vagabond in the forests which are already red and breezy, and where the hunters now chase deer to death, or in the streets in dreary and desolate precincts, or I loiter along the Salzach and watch the gulls (which is still my happiest way of doing nothing).

Georg Trakl to Irene Altmann,
a friend in Vienna, early autumn 1911

The year 1910 was a momentous one in Georg's life and work. The months he had enjoyed having his sister in Vienna came to an end when she left at the end of April to return to Salzburg. The rigors of her music courses, her inability to find any male companionship beyond the platonic and her opium addiction forced a change of scene, and she would henceforth continue her piano studies in Berlin. Her brother reconciled himself to feeling alone in Vienna, which he shared in letters to friends, self-aware, too, that he could rein back on his disturbing '*Stil*', his manner of commenting on himself.

In June, Tobias Trakl died at the age of seventy-four. For long the centre and support of the family, his loss had a devastating effect on Georg and his siblings. Willy, the eldest and now the head of the family, didn't have the business acumen or the patience of his father when it came to the Trakl black sheep: Georg and Grete. For Trakl's poems, however, the image of the father—his corpse and ghost—became an inspiration and more evidence of the prevailing atmosphere of decline, whether personal, familial or imperial. This was especially true in regard to what became the running theme of an unworthy generation, kind, race and even gender—summed up by the German catchall *Geschlecht*. Trakl's poems had always had an air of nostalgia for a Golden Age to which the new century hardly belonged (a world view going far beyond, but in some way not unlike, his mother's collecting and hoarding antiques).

As Trakl found his own voice and moved away from the French Symbolists and German Romantics, the protagonist of his poems became more like ghosts in their apartness (what later so fascinated Heidegger in his reading of Trakl). It is a distance too, a stance that came from his distancing himself not only from his sister but also women in general. Though not sympathetic to the misogyny of Otto Weiniger in *Geschlecht und Charakter* (Sex and Character, 1903), Trakl seems to have replaced the prostitutes of his younger days with the woman counterpart seen by Weininger—independent of men and capable of male striving and genius in his later relationship with Else Lasker-Schüler (Grete's only 'rival'). This sublimation of sexual tension is more apparent in his poems from 1910 on. His lines, too, became ever more discrete, simple and painterly, like the stark images of his friend Kokoschka. Liminal beings begin to populate the poems—angels, demons, dead gods, nymphs, fawns and statues of dead nobles, hunted animals, skeletons, corpses and the ever-shape-shifting presence of the poet and the figure of the sister. And this figure may, indeed, by more of a composite than we know, for Trakl adored his older sisters too.

One has to question just what kind of muse Grete was—and the desire for an answer may begin her own vigorous curiosity. In a letter from mid-1911, Trakl wrote Erhard Buschbeck, passing on Grete's request for his address, something that Trakl felt he could not do so himself without his friend's blessing. Undoubtedly, Trakl wished to spare Buschbeck the kind of letters that he himself received from his sister. These, like much of their correspondence, have been lost or destroyed—and only a few intimations suggest their tenor and contents. To his brother Fritz once, Georg described Grete's letters as 'eccentric Epistles' in which everything was 'the same' with her as though they held no further interest or to suppress it. But what can be surmised with even this little is that Grete's letters to Georg were uncomfortable and distressing to read, something, perhaps, he felt best left to him alone. And if Buschbeck deigned to write Grete, that risked another kind of distress. Trakl asked Buschbeck that he not give her copies of his poems, especially those shared 'in a fit of indiscrimination'. 'God knows,' Trakl wrote, 'what fantastic attempts' his sister would undertake to see them. The aftermath of such an exposure would mean having to explain to her or explain away the 'sister; in the poems, the muse, the love object or the wrong idea.

Despite his ghostly conceits, Georg had to live in a material world and according to the middle-class lifestyle to which he was accustomed. He needed so many crowns for his rent, his clothes, meals, stationery (he was especially fond of good English-made paper), books for his travelling library and the necessities of self-medication—cigarettes, brandy, wine and drugs. He had to make a living and not just the pretence of one. However, it became increasingly more difficult to remain the high-functioning addict and poet–perfectionist, given his constant depressions and manifestations of anti-social and even psychotic behaviours (as when he would implore with friends on some topic with his arms outstretched).

The Imperial-Royal *Landswehr*—the army that served the Austrian territory of the Dual Monarchy—required young men to serve in its reserves. A master's degree (*Magister*) in pharmacy gave Trakl a certain degree of leverage and advantage for his military obligation. In October 1910, he was assigned to the Garrison Hospital 2 in Vienna, where he rose to the rank of a medical assistant with the equivalent rank of lieutenant. There he not only learnt the necessary medical skills to tend wounds and administer drugs on the battlefield but also all the bookkeeping of a properly run hospital pharmacy. It was an amazing accomplishment for a young man who felt himself the victim of his 'continuously fluctuating and despairing nature about everything'. A studio photograph of Trakl, dressed in the crisp blue tunic of a subaltern in the 2nd Landwehr Infantry Regiment, suggests some personal pride, especially given the sword hanging from his belt, so in contrast to the image of a poet–drug addict wielding a syringe to kill his pain and suppress his deliria.

During the second half of 1911, Trakl returned to Salzburg and the White Angel, serving as civilian pharmacist until April 1912 when he was promoted to Garrison Hospital 10 in the provincial capital of Innsbruck. His commanding officer in Vienna wrote a letter of recommendation in which Trakl was described as hard-working, friendly and of a reliable character— all which is in contrast to his letters in which his mood swings to being the opposite. His first impressions of Innsbruck, which, despite the breathtaking beauty around it, left him as disconsolate and estranged as Vienna three years earlier; writing to Buschbeck of his impressions, he mentions the Tirol as another 'brutal' environment and Innsbruck itself as the 'most vulgar city that existed on this encumbered and accursed world'. He could see himself suffering here for a decade and it almost brought him to tears thinking of how hopeless his new situation was. 'What a bother,' he wrote. 'However, I will ever remain a poor Kaspar Hauser'— as though doing so were some sort of survival instinct, a defence mechanism. But like the young Hauser, Trakl attracted attention as a person of interest. He joined a new literary circle around Ludwig von Ficker and his influential journal *Der Brenner*—The Burner, the one who burns, who sets fire.

Von Ficker, an aristocrat as well as editor, was a friend of Alfred Loos and Karl Kraus and knew of Trakl's work when they met. He readily understood his talent, his drug addiction and his mentally fragile state and fulfilled the important role of friend, confidante and mentor. Gradually, Trakl became a fixture at von Ficker's country estate at Mühlau, befriending not only von Ficker's wife and children but also his brother, musicologist Rudolf von Ficker. So much so that he reconciled himself to the surrounding landscape of forests and mountains and even felt at home.

Trakl's regular appearances in *Der Brenner* and von Ficker's tireless enthusiasm for his poetry are why we still read him today. In late 1912, the publisher Kurt Wolff offered to print his first book, simply titled *Poems* (*Gedichte*, 1913), a volume that grew from the same manuscripts, revisions and false starts from which the following poems are taken.

What Trakl demanded of himself as a poet during this time would have a deleterious effect on his ability to work at the garrison hospital. In the autumn of 1912, he resigned because he found his duties too strenuous. Not wanting to be a financial burden on his family and friends, in December he took a position in the Ministry of Public Works but resigned two days later. In the following months, he also worked as an unpaid accounting intern for the War Ministry's pension office before resigning from that post as well. It seemed all he could do now was write poems and letters to his friends and family and his sister in Berlin.

Melusine

Whatever am I waking up for?
My child, blossoms fell during the night!

Who whispers so sadly, like in a dream?
My child, the springtime goes through the room.

O look! His face as though bleached by tears!
My child, he may bloom too profusely.

How my mouth burns! Why am I weeping?
My child, I kiss my life inside you!

Who seizes me so hard, who bows to me?
My child, I am folding your hands for you.

Just where am I going? I dreamt so pretty!
My child, we want to enter heaven.

How nice, how nice! Who smiles so gently?
Thereupon her eyes became white—

Thereupon every light went out
And a deep night gusted through the house.

The Night of the Poor

It gets dark!
And O the night hammers
Dead on our door!
A child whispers:
How you tremble
So much!
Yet we poor bow
Lower and keep silent
And keep silent as if we were no more!

Night Song

Strike me pain! The wound is hot.
I'll pay this torment no mind!
From my wounds behold a star
Bloom full of riddles by night!
Strike me death! For I am done.

De Profundis I

The dead-house is filled with the night
My father sleeps, I hold vigil.

The hard face that the dead assume
Flickers white in the candlelight.

The flowers are fragrant, the flies hum,
My heart listens unfeeling and mute.

The wind knocks softly on the door,
Which opens with a bright rattle.

Outside a field of wheat rustles,
The sun hisses on the vault of heaven.

Orchard and grove hang full of fruit
And birds and butterflies whirl in the air.

In the field the peasants are mowing
In the intense silence of midday.

I make a sign of the cross for the dead
And my steps fade noiseless in the green.

At the Cemetery

Warmed hot the brittle stones loom.
Yellow wisps of incense hover.
Bees hum swarming in disarray
And the flower trellis quivers.

Slowly a procession stirs
Along the sunlight-silenced walls,
Dwindles, flickering like a mirage—
Requiems sift deeply downwards.

It is long heard in the green,
Making the bushes seem brighter;
Brown swarms of mosquito spread
Above the old stones for the dead.

Sunny Afternoon

A branch sways me in the deep blue.
In the mad autumn chaos of leaves
Butterflies flicker, drunk and mad
Axe strokes echo in the meadow.

My mouth smothers itself in red berries
And light and shade play in the foliage.
Golden dust falls for hours on end,
Which hisses into the brown soil.

The thrush is laughing from the bushes
And mad and loud above me whips
The autumn chaos of leaves together—
Fruit breaks off luminous and heavy.

Era

A beast's face in the brown rankness
Glows shyly at me, the bushes gleam.
Quite faraway with children's voices
An old fountain sings. I listen.

The angry jackdaws jeer at me
And all around the birch become blurs.
I stand still for the bonfire of weeds
And quietly therein pictures paint themselves.

On gold soil an ancient love story.
The clouds on the hill spread their silence.
From the ghostly mirror of a pond
Fruit beckons, shining and heavy.

The Shadow

As I sat in the garden this morning—
The trees were standing in blue blossom,
Filled with thrush calling and trilling—
I saw my shadow in the grass,

Utterly contorted, a strange beast,
Which lay like a bad dream before me.

And I walked and shook all over,
While a fountain sang in the blueness
And a bud burst open in crimson
And the beast walked alongside.

Wondrous Spring

Surely it was deep into noon,
I lay upon an ancient stone,
And before me in wondrous garb
There stood three angels in the sunlight.

O spring, season full of portent!
The last snow melted in the field,
And birch's hair hung trembling
In the cold, clear lake.

A blue ribbon fluttered from the sky,
And a cloud flowed lovely within,
The one towards which I lay dreaming—
The angels knelt in the sunlight.

A bird clamoured wondrous tidings,
And I understood it at once:
Before your first desire is stilled,
You must go die, you must go die!

The Dream of an Afternoon

Keep still! the old man comes walking;
And his steps fade away again.
Shadows float above and below—
Birches, which hang in the window.

And on the ancient grape-vined hill
The faun's reel gambols around once more,
And the willowy nymphs ascend
Softly from the well's reflection.

Hear that! a distant storm threatens.
Incense smoulders from the dark cress,
Butterflies celebrate silent Masses
At a fallen flower trellis.

Summer Sonata

The rotten fruit smells deafening.
Bush and tree resound with sunlight,
Swarming clusters of black flies sing
At the brown clearing in the woods.

In the deep blueness of the pond
The light of weed fires is ablaze.
From yellow walls of flowers hear
Cries of love suddenly flutter.

Butterflies chase each other long;
In sweltering meadows of thyme
My shadow dances about drunk.
Rapturous blackbirds chirp brightly.

Clouds expose their unyielding breasts,
And bedecked by leaves and berries
You see grinning in the dark pines
A skeleton play violin.

Lucent Hour

Pipes playing far on the hill.
Fauns are lurking in the marshes,
Hidden in the reeds and grass,
The slender nymphs lie languorous.

Golden butterflies delight,
In the looking glass of a pond,
Quietly in velvet grass
A beast with two backs rears up.

With a sob in the birch grove
Orpheus tenderly lisps of love.
Softly and flirtingly join
The nightingales in his song.

Phoebus a flame still gutters
At the mouth of Aphrodite
And jets of ambergris inside—
The hour darkly reddens.

Childhood Memory

The sun shines lonely in the afternoon,
And the sound of bees softly drifts away.
In the garden whisper the sisters' voices—
As the boy in the wooden shed listens

Still feverishly over book and plate.
The weary lindens wilt immersed in blue.
Drowned in the ether a heron hangs motionless,
By the fence a grand show of shadows plays.

The sisters enter the house silent,
And soon after their white frocks shimmer
Uncertainly from radiant rooms,
And the bushes' wild roar dies down.

The boy is caressing the cat's fur,
Enthralled by the reflection in her eyes.
Far on the hill an organ's sound heaves
Gloriously into the sky.

An Evening

The sky was overcast in the evening.
And through the grove full of silence and grief,
Travels a darkly golden shower.
Evening bells faded off in the distance.

The earth has partaken of ice-cold waters,
At the forest edge a fire set dies away,
The wind sang low with angelic voices
And shivering I have gone down on my knees,

Amid the heather, in the bitter cress.
Way out there somewhere in silver pools floated
Clouds, forlorn keepers of the watch over love.
The heath was lonely and immeasurable.

Season

Veins of ruby trailed in the leaves.
Then the fishpond was still and wide.
At the forest's edge lay scattered
A bluish dapple and brown dust.

A fisherman hauled in his net.
Then twilight came over a field.
Yet a farm still seemed palely lit
And maidservants brought fruit and wine.

Later a far shepherd's song died.
Then cottages stood stark and strange.
The forest under a grey shroud
Awakened a sad memory.

And overnight time turned quiet
And as if into black holes flew
A ravens' host through the forest,
Making for the city's far bells.

In the Wine Country

The sun paints the yard and walls with autumn,
The fruit, layered in heaps all around,
Before which pitiful children cower.
A gust of wind clears ancient lindens.

A golden shower rains through the gateway
And resting tired on rotten benches
Are the women, whose bellies are blessed.
The drunkards are waving glass and cup.

A vagabond lets his fiddle sound
And skirts billow wanton in the dance.
Hard brown bodies twine around each other.
From the windows there watch empty eyes.

Stench rises from the well's reflection.
And black, fallen and solitary,
The grape-vined hills all around grow dim.
A line of birds streaks swiftly southwards.

Colourful Autumn

A fountain sings. The clouds stack up
Into the clear blue, ones white, wispy.
People slowly promenade hushed
Through the old garden in the evening.

The marbles of ancestors grey.
Passing birds stretch into the distance.
A faun with dead eyes contemplates
Shadows slipping into the darkness.

The leaves fall red from an old tree
And spiral through an open window.
Firelight flares in a room and paints
Chaotic fearsome apparitions.

An opalish haze weaves over the grass
A carpet of dead redolences.
In the fountain like green glass shimmers
The sickle moon in the freezing wind.

The Dark Valley

A flock of crows scatters into the pines
And green evening mists are gathering
And like a dream a sound of violins
And girls running to dance in a tavern.

One hears the drunkards' laughter and shouting,
A shiver goes through ancient yew trees.
Flashing across corpse-pale window panes
The shadows of the dancers hurry by.

There is a smell of wine and thyme
And lonely calls echo through the woods.
The beggar folk listen on the steps
And pointlessly begin to pray.

A deer bleeds out in the hazel bushes.
Giant colonnades of trees dully sway,
Overburdened by the wintery clouds.
Lovers lie in embrace by the pond.

Summer Half-Light

Just now a star gleams in the green ether
And they smell the morning in the hospital.
The thrush madly trills hidden in the bush
And cloister bells travel dreamlike and far.

A statue looms in the square, lone and lean,
And red pillows of flowers dawn in courtyards.
From wood balconies the air quivers with heat
And flies quietly swirl around the stench.

The silver curtains before the window
Conceals entangled limbs, lips and tender breasts.
A harsh hammering echoes from the spire's scaffolds
And the moon in heaven's vault wanes white.

A ghostly piecework of dreams shines its last
And monks emerge from the portals of the church
And march away lost into infinity.
A bright summit towers high overhead.

In the Moonlight

A horde of vermin, of mice, rats, rampages
Through the hallway which shimmers in the moonlight.
The wind cries and whimpers as if in a dream.
In the window tremble shadows of small leaves.

Every so often birds chirp in the branches
And spiders go crawling across the bare walls.
Pale flecks shower through the empty corridors.
A curious silence dwells within the house.

Lights appear to slip away in the courtyard
On rotten wood, fallen objects of no use.
After that a star glitters in a black pond.
Figures still stand here from ages long ago.

The contours of other things can still be seen
And a legend, fading on mouldy shields,
Perhaps too the colours in serene images:
Angels, who sing before the throne of Mary.

Allegory

Skyrockets sparkle in yellow sunshine;
In the old park what a masklike multitude.
The landscapes are mirrored in the grey sky.
And sometimes the faun's ghastly scream is heard.

His golden grin appears bright in the grove.
A mêlée of bees is raging in the cress,
A rider canters past on a pale grey horse.
The poplars are blazing in their vague rows.

The girl-child, who had drowned in the pond today,
Is at peace, a saint inside a stark chamber
And often a ray through the clouds dazzles her.

In the hothouse, the old walk listless and sick
And water their flowers, which withered away.
At the gate whisper dream-bewildered voices.

A Spring Evening

Come evening, friend, casting my brow in darkness,
Gliding along paths through soft green seedlings.
Too the willows beckon solemn and grave;
A beloved voice whispers in the tendrils.

A fair wind washes up loveliness from somewhere,
A smell of narcissi, whose silver meets you.
The blackbird makes music in the hazel bush—
From the firs a shepherd's song gives the response.

How long ago has that little house been gone,
Where a little grove of birch trees rains down;
The pond bears a lone figure in the stars—
And shadows, which lap around still in goldness!

And thus is time considered miraculous,
Such that one can seek angels with human eyes,
Which delight in a game not full of guilt.
Yes! Thus is time considered miraculous.

Lamentation

The friend, she flutters with her green flowers,
Performs in a lunar gardens—
O! What glows behind the yew hedge!
A golden mouth stirring my lips,
And they echo like the stars
Above the brook of Kidron.
But stellar clouds descend across the plain,
Wild and unspeakable dances.
O! My friend your lips,
Pomegranate lips,
Ripen on my crystal shell's mouth.
The golden silence of the plain
Lies heavy upon us.
Into the sky the blood reeks,
That of Herod's
Murdered children.

Spring of the Soul

Flowers scattered blue and white
Strive merrily in the ground.
The evening hour weaves silver,
A mild bleakness, solitude.

Life blooms now full of danger,
Sweet peace around cross and grave.
A bell's heralding the end,
All of it seems wonderful.

Willows float in the ether,
Here and there a light flickers.
Spring whispers and promises
And the wet ivy trembles.

Bread and wine grow a rich green,
An organ swells with wondrous force.
And around cross and passion
A ghostly brilliance shines.

O! How lovely are these days.
Children go through the twilight;
Already the wind blows bluer.
A thrush call mocks from afar.

Half-Light in the West

A faun's scream comes bounding through sparks,
In parks cascades of light send up spume,
A metallic haze about the steel arcades
Of the city, which wheels around the sun.

A tiger-drawn god speeds shining
On past the women and bright bazaars
Filled with flowing gold and goods and wares.
And a slave race wails now and then.

A drunken ship turns sluggishly
In green sunbeams on the canal.
A brilliant concert of colours
Strikes up faint near the hospital

Some Quirinal projects a sombre pomp.
Colourful crowds circle in mirrors
Upon the bridge arches and rails.
A demon keeps pale watch outside the banks.

A dreamer sees pregnant women
Gliding on by in a lustre of slime,
A dying man hears the bells tolling—
A gold hoard glows softly in the grey.

The Church

Painted angels keep watch over the altars;
And quiet and shadows; a ray from blue eyes.
In clouds of incense shimmers dirty soap water.
Shapes shamble mournfully in the emptiness.

With her faded dead cheeks a child prostitute
Looks like the Madonna at a black prayer bench.
Wax figures ride upon golden shafts of light;
Moon and sun revolve around a white-bearded God.

A lustre of smooth pillars and skeletons.
The sweet voices of the boys died in the choir.
Very quietly lost colours start to move,
A streaming red from Mary Magdalene's lips.

A pregnant woman goes astray in bad dreams
Through this twilight, which is full of masks, banners.
Her shadow crosses the still orbits of saints,
The peace of the angels in their whitewashed realms.

To Angela

1

A solitary fate in deserted rooms.
A gentle madness touches their wallpaper.
Crimson geranium beds at the windows,
Narcissus too, and withered more virginal
Than alabaster, which gleam in the garden.

India's mornings cast smiles in blue veils.

Their sweet incense drives away the stranger's cares,
Sleepless night by the pond around Angela.
His pain rests concealed inside an empty mask,
Thoughts stealing away blackly into the dark.

All around the thrushes laugh from velvet throats.

2

Surrounded by spiked grass, the tired reapers sit
At the crossroad getting drunk from the poppies,
The sky has sunk very heavy upon them,
The milk and desolation of long noon bells.
And sometimes the crows flutter up from the rye.

The hot earth increases with fruit and horrors

In a golden glow, O the childish posture
Of carnality, its hyacinthine silence,
As bread and wine, fed on the flesh of the earth,
Reveal their spirit to Sebastian dreaming.

Angela's ghost belongs to the fleecy clouds.

3

The fruits, which grow round and red in the branches,
This angel's lips, which manifest her sweetness,
Like nymphs, which are leaning out over the spring
In long hours of regard filled with tranquillity,
The long green-golden hours of the afternoon.

But sometimes the ghost turns to games and contest.

A battle's tumult surges through golden clouds
Of flies above the gangrene and abscesses.
A demon thinks of storms in the sultry air,
In the sepulchral shade of sad cypresses.

Then the first lightning bolt falls from black forges.

4

The silver whispering of the willow grove;
A rain lingers long in the strains of a flute.

How the birds hover motionless with evening!
A blue water's sleeping in the branches' dark;
It is the poet who is this beauty's priest.

Meditations filled with pain in the dark chill.

Soft pillows scented by poppies and incense
At the forest's edge and the shadow of despair
Angela's joy and the games the stars play
The night swallows up the lovers' languishing.

The forest's edge and the shadow of despair.

Reverie in the Evening

Where one walks with evening, is not the angel's shadow
And the beautiful! Grief varies with milder forgetting;
The stranger's hands touch the coolness and the cypresses
And an astonishing exhaustion seizes his soul.

The marketplace is empty of red fruit and garlands.
The church's black pomp makes for one harmonious voice,
In a garden resonate the sounds of gentle play,
Where the tired gather together after dinner.

A carriage rushes, a brook very far through green pools.
There a childhood revealed itself dreamlike and flowed on,
Angela's stars, clasped piously in a mystical image,
And the cool of the evening quietly takes its form.

For one alone in thought, white poppies release his limbs,
Such that he beholds righteousness and God's profound joy.
His shadow wanders out of the garden in white silk
And bends down low over water full of sombreness.

Branches thrust whisperingly into a forlorn room
And lovemaking and a brief shake of evening flowers.
Grain and golden grapevines gird the place of humankind,
Nevertheless a lunar cast gives thought to the dead.

Winter Path in A Minor

Often these red globes emerge from the branches,
The long snowfall blankets softly and black.
The priest provides the dead with a cortege.
The nights fill with the revels of masquerades.

Later wind-tossed crows sweep over the village;
In books fairy tales read wonderfully.
At the window an old man's hair flutters.
Demons make their passage through the diseased soul.

The well freezes in the courtyard. In the dark
A wrecked staircase plunges and a wind blows
Through these ancient shafts, which are filled with earth.
The palate savours the strong spice of the frost.

Ever Darker

The wind, which stirs the crimson treetops
Is God's breath, which comes and goes.
The black village rises up before the forest;
Three shadows are laid across the field.

Below and still the valley grows dark
To one modest sparingly.
An austereness greets in garden and hall,
Which wishes for the day to end.

Pious and dark an organ's tone.
There Mary sits enthroned in her blue robe
And rocks her little baby in her hand.
The night is star-bright and long.

Afoot

A smell of myrrh, which wanders through twilight.
A Shrovetide play, on squares black and desert.
A golden beam breaks through the clouds and streams
Into small shops dreamy and in a daze.

Ruin gleams in soap water and the wind's
Droning call wakes the pain of scorched gardens.
People possessed hurry after dark things.
In the windows dryads rest slim and lithe.

A boy's smile, which is consumed by a wish.
The old doors of a church are staring locked.
Sonatas get a sympathetic ear;
A horseman hurries past on a white steed.

In the gloom an old man trips puppet-like
And a jingle of coins laughs lustily.
A halo falls on that little girl outside
Waiting at the coffeehouse meek and white.

O that golden glow she wakes in the panes!
A sun-filled din booms far and in raptures.

A hunched-over writer smiles as though mad
At the horizon, scared green by turmoil.

In the evening coaches are pulled through storms,
A corpse falls through the dark, empty and pale,
A bright steamboat docks along the canal,
A black girl calls in the savage greenness.

Sleepwalkers step before a candlelight,
The evil spirit fares in a spider.
A seat of pestilence circles the drinkers;
An oak forest bursts inside bleak salons.

An old opera house appears on the plain.
Undreamt-of masks surge through the narrow lanes,
And somewhere a fire still burns furiously.
The bats squeak in the roaring of the wind.

Rented rooms loom filled with despair and stench.
Shades of violet and harmonies stretch on
Before the hungry at their cellar doors.
A sweet child is sitting dead on a bench.

December Sonnet

With evening a troupe leaves through the forest
On fantastical wagons, little horses.
A hoard of gold seems locked away in the clouds.
Villages are painted in the white plain.

The red wind fills the linen black and cold.
A dog rots, a bush smoulders sprinkled with blood.
The reeds are watered by a yellow horror
And a cortege slowly winds to the graveyard.

The old man's hut fades close by in the grey,
A glow of ancient treasures shines in the pond.
The peasants sit down to wine at the inn.

A boy slides timorously towards a woman.
A monk fades in the darkness soft and sombre.
A leafless tree is a sleeper's sacristan.

Poems, 1912–1914

I am like a dead man passing an echo, passing a black city, which rushed through me like an inferno through one damned.

I walk through a loud, beautiful sun in Mühlau and I am still reeling.

Veronal has given me some sleep beneath Kokoschka's Franziska.[*]

Georg Trakl to Erhard Buschbeck, early January 1913

[*] A poster of the title character of *Das Mysterium Franciska* (The Mystery of Francesa) by Frank Wedekind, which Oskar Kokoschka designed in 1912.

As a youth, during the summer of 1903, Trakl had lived with relatives in Ödenburg. The loneliness he experienced there is found in the prose piece 'Dreamland', but why his parents sent him away can only be conjectured, at best read into the strange, one-sided love story of the young narrator for his dying cousin. Grete was nearly twelve and home from her Catholic boarding school in St Pölten. Did her mother have some reason to keep her sexually mature, precocious and difficult sixteen-year-old son apart from her youngest daughter? One possible answer, which is believed to date from July 1903, is on the back of an envelope where Trakl transcribed a lyric poem by Nikolaus Lenau titled 'Question (*Frage*)' and undersigned it 'Your dear brother Georg'.

Lenau's inquiry is posed to the human heart—What is it that makes you happy? The answer is: 'An unrepeatable moment.' It means at once what cannot be spoken and what cannot, or should not, be reprised. Five years later, in 1908, Trakl wrote an aphorism that may stand as a resolution to this paradox, that he would have to distance himself from whatever the 'moment' was: 'Only to he who scorns happiness comes insight.'

In early April 1913, Kurt Wolff assigned the reading of Trakl's manuscript of poems to another young poet, Franz Werfel, the editor of the publishing house's new anthology of Expressionist poetry, *Der jüngste Tag*—Judgement Day. Although charged with the close reading of many manuscripts, and more inclined to spend time on his own verse and departing for a holiday on Lake Garda, Werfel 'made a selection from the Trakl' for the anthology and reported back to Wolff that he was 'very much in favour of your publishing the whole book at some point'. Soon after, Trakl received a contract for *Poems*.

Elated, a burst of hurried productivity followed in May and June to finalize the manuscript and check proofs. Trakl's correspondence with his new publisher in Leipzig reveals his desire to include his latest poems that he found appropriate for his first book, revisions to various lines and the care taken in arranging each poem to unfold one after the other. Trakl urged Buschbeck, as the president of the Vienna's Society of Art and Literature, to provide a list of subscribers who would purchase the first edition. By the end of June, however, Trakl's enthusiasm for his book was overshadowed by a bout of depression which began when Adolf Loos failed to meet him at the train station in Vienna, so as to join him for a pleasant, companionable journey to Salzburg. Trakl even waited in the dining car in vain for Loos, only to arrive at his destination on a summer day as 'cloudy and cold as any other and raining without interruption'. Trakl, in a letter to von Ficker, described the crushing sense of disappointment that enveloped him:

> Now and them a sunbeam falls from those last sunny
> Innsbruck days into this dismalness and fills me with
> the deepest gratitude for you and those fine people

whose goodness I, in truth, don't really deserve. Too little love, too little justice and mercy, and always too little love, all too much hardness, pride and all manner of criminality—this is me. I am certain that I simply omitted evil out of weakness and cowardice and with that am still guilty of my wickedness. I long for the day when my soul will no longer have to live or be able to in this polluted body filthy with despair, when it will leave behind this mocking shape of shit and foulness, which is simply an all too true mirror image of this godless, cursed century.

'[T]his is me'? Trakl's question is self-referential, but in what way? His half-brother had to pay his debts, Grete's and those of their late father. Such a financial burden may have been impressed on Georg when he came home. An argument over money may be the only source of the disappointment Trakl expressed in his letter. However, in a letter to Buschbeck written before the Salzburg visit, Trakl had asked if his friend had seen Grete there, which can be interpreted three ways: that he had expected her in June, suffered missing her—or, indeed, having to avoid her. What is known is that Georg's relationship with his sister had changed. In the previous year, Grete had married a man in his fifties, old enough to be her father. Initially, Georg, like the rest of her family, knew little about the husband, Arthur Langen. On the surface, he seemed respectable enough as a member of petty aristocracy and the nephew of Grete's landlady in Berlin. Since the 1890s, he had worked variously as a minor publisher, theatre impresario, playwright and a municipal civil servant and tax collector. However, he had little of note to show for his efforts, even after he purchased the rights to stage the plays of Oscar

Wilde in Germany. Thus, Willy, as Grete's ward, was naturally suspicious of Langen's intentions of helping Grete become a concert pianist. The Trakl family had long paid for Grete to live and study in Berlin under Ernst von Dohnányi and there was no evidence that Langen had any experience in music or intended to assume any of the financial burden for Grete. Willy also suspected sexual immorality of the fiancé, such that Langen had to send a photograph to show that he did look acceptable (and not 'old and senile') as well as a medical report to prove that he had no venereal disease. He also hired a detective to vouch for his character as not someone who would attach himself to Grete as a parasite. Since Langen had never married before, there would be suspicions that he was a homosexual. Grete was summoned back to Salzburg after Willy refused to give her permission to marry. Langen, however, successfully sued the Trakl family and the April–October couple married just weeks before the bride turned twenty.

Georg seemed to take no side in the marriage. If he had any reason to feel contrary, it was over his poems, for Langen wanted to publish a selection, perhaps obtained from Grete, in yet another of his ventures, an anthology under his imprint. And if Georg had any reason to be supportive of the April–October couple, it involved a kind of venture on his part, which his friend, the writer Karl Röck, recorded in his diary years later, after Georg and Grete were gone:

> Trakl once spoke of the 'repressed sexual feelings, between brother and sister, of the most doomed relationship, a relationship of ruin', of a 'relationship for fairy tales and myths of downfall'. Because the brother,

'the finest of procurers', can suffer no other sexual relationship for the cherished object of his desire. He always releases the sister to another man and never her choice. The beloved becomes nothing but a deal with a real businessman, as goods sold.

Indeed, Langen was such 'businessman'. Even before their marriage, he saw himself as Grete's promoter and engaged a new teacher for her, Richard Buhlig, a young American of German descent living in Berlin. His expertise not only included the traditional piano repertoire of Beethoven and the like but also obscure Baroque and the latest avant-garde music. He had performed the world premiere of Schoenberg's Three Piano Pieces and had a list of prominent students that began when he was an instructor at the Institute of Musical Art (now the Juilliard School) in New York City

The pairing was a good match and, in September 1912, Grete not only impressed Buhlig with her musical talents, she also sent him a thick envelope—discovered by Grete's biographer—with a manuscript of poems treated in a very strange way. The typed copies are cut off at the bottom to remove any attribution, save for one sheet, an unknown poem titled 'Elenden' (Miserables) with only the topmost parts of the tallest letters missed by the scissors. Other poems are copied in Grete's hand.

[*Nearness of Death*]

For a long time the monk listens to the dying bird at the
      forest's edge[,]
O the nearness of death, the bone place on a hill[,]
The cold sweat which appears on the waxen brow.
The white shadow of the brother, who runs down the narrow
      pass.

The evening has gone in the dark villages of childhood[.]
The pond beneath the willows
Is filling with the red guldens of a sad autumn.

O the fat rats in the straw!
The blind man, who again with evening stands on the path[.]
The stillness of grey clouds has fallen on the field.

Spiders hang in the white caves of despair
While the crimson of his nocturnal days sinks away
From the bone hands of one alone—
Quietly the brother's lunar eyes.

O already in cooler pillows
Yellow with incense part the lovers' slender limbs.

[A tapestry, in which the stricken landscape pales]

A tapestry, in which the stricken landscape pales[,]
Perhaps Galilee, a small boat in the storm[.]
Golden objects are raining down from the thunderheads[,]
The madness that seizes the gentle man.
The ancient waters gurgle with blue laughter.

And sometimes a dark shaft will open up.
The possessed are reflected in cold metals[.]
Drops of blood are falling on glowing slabs
And a face rots away during a black night.
Banners, which loll in the gloom of vaulted ceilings.

Someone else remembers the flight of birds[,]
The mystical signs of the crows above the gallows[.]
Coppery snakes become lost in the spiked grass[.]
In pillows of incense a smile whorish and sly.

Good Friday's children blindly stand by the fences[.]
In the mirror of dark drains filled with decay[,]
The dying's sighing onwards with getting well
And angels who make their way through white eyes[.]
From their lids lowers a golden salvation.

[*Pink mirror: an ugly image*]

Pink mirror: an ugly image,
Which appears in the black background,
Blood is weeping from broken eyes[.]
A blasphemer plays with dead snakes.

Snow trickles through the matted shirt
Crimson over the black face,
Which breaks into massive fragments
Of planets, dead and strange.

A spider appears in the black background[,]
Ecstasy, your face dead and strange.
Blood trickles through the matted shirt[.]
Snow is weeping from broken eyes.

[Darkness is the song of the spring rain during the night]

Darkness is the song of the spring rain during the night,
Underneath the clouds the showers of pink pear blossoms[,]
Trickery of the heart, song and madness of the night.
Fiery angels, who appear from departed eyes.

[A shape which long dwelt in the coolness of dark stone]

A shape which long dwelt in the coolness of dark stone
Opens resounding the pale mouth[,]
Wide owl eyes—resounding gold.

These found the den of the forest in ruin and empty[,]
The shadow of a doe in the rotten branches[,]
At the edge of the spring, the darkness of his childhood.

Long sings a bird of your downfall at the forest's edge[,]
The fearful shiver of your brown cloak;
The shadow of the owl appears in the rotten branches.

Long sings a bird of your downfall at the forest's edge[,]
The fearful shiver of your brown cloak[;]
The shadow of the mother appears in the spiked grass.

Long sings a bird of your downfall at the forest's edge[,]
The fearful shiver of your brown cloak[;]
The shadow of the black horse appears in the mirror
    of the stream.

[*Going Down*]

With evening, when we walk home through golden summers
The shadows of joyous saints are with us.
The vines softly green around, the grain yellows
O my brother, what peace is in the world.
We dive embracing into brown water,
The dark grotto of manly despair[.]
On barren paths cross the journeys of the festering,
But we rest the beatified in the setting sun.
Peace, where the colours of autumn illuminate[.]
Overhead the walnut trees rustle with our former lives

Delirium

The black snow, which trickles from the rooftops;
A red finger plunges into your forehead,
In the bare room the blue glaciers descend,
Which are slowly dying mirrors of lovers.
In heavy slabs the head breaks and contemplates
The shadows inside the glass of blue glaciers,
The cold smile of a dead prostitute.
The evening wind weeps in clouds of carnations.

At the Rim of an Old Fountain

Dark reading of the water: a broken forehead in the mouth
     of the night,
The blue shadow of a boy sighing into black pillows,
The rustling of the maples, footsteps in the old park,
Chamber concerts, which fade upon a winding staircase,
Perhaps a moon, which quietly climbs the steps.
The soft voices of the nuns in the ruined church,
A blue tabernacle that slowly opens up,
Stars that fall into your bone hands,
Perhaps a path through abandoned rooms,
The blue tone of the flute in the hazel bushes—ever so quiet.

Along Walls

There is an old pathway which goes
Along wild gardens and lonely walls.
Thousand-year-old yew trees shiver
In the rising, falling song of the wind.

Butterflies dance as though they would soon die,
My gaze drinks weeping the shadows and lights.
Faraway float women's faces
Painted ghostly in the blue.

A smile is trembling in the sunshine,
While I continue walking slowly;
Unending love provides the escort.
The hard stone turns quietly to green.

Quietly

A black wind is thundering in the stubble.
The sadness' violet colours come into bloom,
Circling thoughts, which sombrely surround the brain,
Alongside the fence lean asters, which have died,
And blackish and weather-beaten sunflowers,
Dissolved in rouges and shades of cyan.
A curious sound of bells quivers through
Mignonettes, which have died in black crape ribbon
And our foreheads, lattice-worked by the shadows,
Quietly sink down into shades of cyan
With blackish and weather-beaten sunflowers
And brown asters, which have died along the fence.

In the Hospital

The clock, which tolls twelve deep in the greening—
A bright horror seizes the fevered patients,
The sky glitters and the gardens are storming.
A waxen face looks up in the window.

Perhaps so that this hour will stand still.
Colourful images flit before glazed eyes
In the pitch and roll of ships on the river.
A flock of nuns breezes by on the stairs.

And clouds begin to stir in the blue wind,
As if they were lovers embracing in sleep.
Perhaps so flies swarm around a carcass there,
Perhaps too a child weeps in mother's lap.

At the window flowers wilt warm and red,
Which were brought to the beautiful boy today.
How he lifted his hands and quietly laughed.
There prayers were said. Perhaps someone lies dead.

It seems that a dreadful shriek is heard too
And faces seen swimming in a sultry mist.

A piano piece sounds dead from bright rooms.
Just then the clock strikes three in the deep green.

From there a black procession floats back.
Then one hears chorales still ringing from far off.
Perhaps so angels sing in the hall as well.
In the garden white poppies stream dreamlike.

[*Something pale, lying in the shadows of a falling staircase*]

1

Something pale, lying in the shadows of a falling staircase—
Which arches up at night in a silver form
And wanders beneath the cloister walk.

In the coolness of a tree and without pain
The perfect breathes
And has no need of the autumn stars—

Thorns, over which that other falls.
Lovers long
Contemplate his sad fall.

[The stillness of the departed loves the old garden]

The stillness of the departed loves the old garden[,]
The madwoman who dwelt in blue rooms,
With evening her still figure appears in the window

But she lowered the yellowed curtain—
The sliding of glass beads reminds us of our childhood,
At night we found a black moon in the forest[.]

In a mirror's blueness echoes the soft sonata[,]
Long embraces[,]
Your smile glides across the dying's mouth.

[With pink steps the stone descends into the moor]

With pink steps the stone descends into the moor
A song of gliding away and black laughter
In rooms the figures exit and enter
And Death in a black skiff gives a bone smile.

In red wine a pirate on the canal
Whose mast and sail often parted in the storm.
The drowned are battered crimson by the stonework
Of the bridge. The sentry's cry rattles of steel.

Yet sometimes the eye in candlelight hears
And follows the shadows along falling walls
And there are dancers with hands entwined in sleep.

The night, which blackly crashes at your head
And the dead, who turn themselves round in their beds
To take hold of the marble with broken hands.

[*The blue night has softly risen upon our foreheads*]

The blue night has softly risen upon our foreheads.
Quietly our decayed hands touch.
Sweet bride!

Our faces became white, lunar pearls
Melted into the bed of a green pond.
Turned stone we watch our stars.

O who suffer! Guilty ones walk in the garden,
The shadows in wild embrace,
Such that tree and beast in towering fury sank away over them.

Soft harmonies, as we fare in crystal waves
Through the still night
A pink angel steps outside the graves of lovers.

[*O living in the stillness of the darkening garden*]

O living in the stillness of the darkening garden,
As the sister's eyes opened wide and dark in the brother,
The crimson of their agonized mouths
Melted away in the cool of evening.
Heart-rending hour.

September ripened the golden pears. Sweetness of incense
And the dahlias blaze along the old fence
Admit! where we were, when we drew by in a black boat
During the evening,

The crane flew overhead. The freezing arms
Kept embracing blackness, and within blood ran.
And moist blue down our temples. Poor little children.
From knowing eyes a dark kind is deep in thought.

With Evening

A blue brook, a path, and an evening there by falling cottages.
Behind dark bushes children play with blue and red balls;
A few shift their brows and hands rot in the brown leaves.

In this silence of bone the heart of the lonely glows,
A small boat drifts on blackish water.
Through a dark grove hair flutters and the brown maids'
    laughter.

The shadows of the old ones cross the flight of a small bird;
A secret of blue flowers upon their temples.
Others sway back and forth on black benches in the evening
    wind.

Golden signs softly extinguish in the bare branches
Of the chestnuts; a crash from the dark cymbals of summer,
When the stranger appears on the collapsing stairs

Summer

Summer under whitewashed arches,
Yellowed wheat, a bird which flies in and out
Evening and the dark fragrance of the green.
A red man, on a darkening path, to where?
Across lonely hills, past the bone house,
Across the ascent of the forest dances the silver heart.

December

The coat in the black wind; the dry reeds quietly whisper
In the stillness of the moor. A flock of wild birds
Follows in the grey sky—
Crosswise over dark waters.

Bone hands glide through the bare birch trees.
The footstep snaps in a brown grove
Where a lone beast dwells to die.

Old women cross the road
Into the village. Spiders fell from their eyes
And red snow. Crows and the long peal of bells

Floated along the black path, Endymion's smile
And lunar slumber
And the metal brow feels its way freezing through the hazel
    bush[.]

Stop expecting the evening in the tavern[,]
Dwelling in a crimson den of wine,
The drunken shadow silently slips from the wallpaper.

For hours a snow made of hair falls at the window
The night chases the sky with black flags and broken masts.

Judgement

Childhood's cottages are in autumn,
A fallen hamlet; apocalyptic shapes,
Singing mothers in the evening wind;
The Angelus at a window and hands clasped.

Stillborn birth; upon a green mound
Mystery and silence of blue flowers.
The crimson mouth opens from madness:
Dies Irae—grave and silence.

Feeling along by the green thorns;
In sleep: hawking blood, hunger and laughter;
Fire in the village, awaking in the green;
Fear and rocking aboard a skiff awash.

Or against a wooden staircase leans
The stranger's white shadow once again.—
Yearning in the blue a poor sinner
Leave his foulness to lilies and rats.

Evening Glass

A child with brown hair. A footstep frightens off
Blackish flames in the damp chill of evening,
Inside a frame of dark golden sunflowers;
A gentle beast sinks upon a red pillow.

A shadow glides like bone across the surface
And quietly from the blue asters' silence
Emerges a red mouth, a riddle-filled seal,
And black eyes are gleaming from the branches

Of the maples whose insane red is blinding.
A gentle body has left the wall behind,
A blue radiance ending with the nightfall.
The wind quietly rattles in empty streets.

At the open window the hour of lovers
Withers away. The clouds of daring journeys
Are accompanied by the path of the lone.
A look drops silver into the brown garden.

The water's dark motion touches the hands.
A meek ghost ages in crystal, clarity.
The birds in flight are untold, a gathering
With the dying; those the dark years follow.

A Sister's Garden

Already it's become cold, become late,
Already it's become autumn
In a sister's garden, soft and still,
Her footsteps have become white.
A blackbird call wanders and late,
Already it's become autumn
In a sister's garden, soft and still;
An angel has become.

On the Hill

In stillness at the edge of the woods slips away
A dark deer
On the hill the evening wind ends quietly,

Soon the blackbird's lament trails off,
And the pipes of autumn
Fall silent in the reeds.

With silver thorns
The frost whips us,
Dying we leant over our graves[.]

Above blue clouds disband;
From black decay
God's radiant angels appear[.]

[*Hohenburg*]

Empty and dead the father's house,
Dark hour
And an awakening in the darkening garden.

Ever do you think the white face of man,
Far from the fury of time;
Green branches bow willingly over something dreaming;

Cross and dusk,
The plangent is clasped in the crimson arms of his star
And the tolling of blue flowers[.]

[*Wind, white voice, which whispers at the drunkard's temples*]

Wind, white voice, which whispers at the drunkard's temples;
Rotting path. Long evening bells drowned in the muck of
    the pond
And over it the yellow flowers of summer droop; with mad
    faces flutter
The bats.

Home! Evening pink mountains! Rest! Purity!
The cry of vultures! Only the sky darkens,
The head drops enormous at the forest's edge.
The night rises out of a black sobbing.

Sunflowers like children flutter around the sleeper awaking.

[So quietly toll]

So quietly toll
The blue shadows with evening
Along the white wall.
The autumnal year declines in stillness.

Hour of interminable despair,
As I suffered death for you.
There blows from the stars
A snowy wind through your hair.

Dark songs
Your crimson mouth sings in me,
The silent cottage of our childhood,
Forgotten fables;

I live like a gentle deer
In the crystal ripple
Of the cool spring
And the violets bloomed all around

[*The dew of spring, which falls from dark branches*]

The dew of spring, which falls from dark branches,
The night comes
With starry shafts, for you forget the light.

Beneath the thorned arch you lay and the needle buries
Itself deep in your crystal body
So that the soul weds the night fierier.

The bride has garlanded herself with stars,
The pure myrtle
Which bends over the adoring face of the dead.

Filled with a blossoming awe
The mistress finally surrounds you in her blue cloak.

[*O the leaf-stripped beeches and the blackish snow*]

O the leaf-stripped beeches and the blackish snow.
The north blows about quietly. Here on the brown path
Went a darkness moons ago.

Alone in the autumn. Ever do the flurries fall
In the bare branches[;]
In the dry reeds; green crystal sings in the pond[.]

Empty the cottage of straw; the tossing birches
Are a childish thing in the night wind.
O the way which quietly freezes in the darkness.
And that place to live in pink snow[.]

Wanderer's Sleep

The white night ever leans against the rock
Where the pines loom in silver tones
Are stone and stars.

The bone footbridge arches over the mountain torrent[,]
The dark shape of the chill follows the sleeper,
A sickle moon in a pink gorge.

Faraway from sleeping herdsmen. In ancient rocks
The toad watches from crystal eyes
The florid wind wakes, the silver voice
Of the deathlike.

Quietly telling the forgotten legend of the forest
The white face of the angel[,]
Quietly the [. . .] water's foam caresses his knee[.]

A pink bud[,]
The one singing's sad mouth of a bird.
A beautiful glow dawns on his brow

Stone and star[,]
Therein the white stranger dwelt long ago.

Along Walls

Nevermore the golden face of spring;
Dark laughter in the hazel bushes. Evening walk in the woods
And the fervent cry of the blackbird.
Daylong the glowing green rustles in the soul of the stranger.

Metal minute: Noon, desolation of summer;
The shadows of the beeches and the yellow grain.
Baptism in chaste waters. O the crimson man.
But forest, pond and white deer are like him.

Cross and church in the village. In dark conversation
Husband and wife knew who each other were
And at a bare wall one alone wanders with his stars.

Quietly across the moon-brightened path of the forest
The wilderness of forgotten chases.
A look of blueness breaks from fallen rocks.

To Novalis

Reposed in crystal earth, a holy stranger,
From that dark mouth a god chose his lament,
When he sank away in his full bloom
The plucking of strings peacefully died
In his breast,
And the spring spread its palms before him
When he with hesitant steps
Abandoned the nighted house in silence.

Hour of Grief

The footsteps blackly in the autumnal garden
Follow the brilliant moon,
The enormous night sinks by a freezing wall.
O, the thorned hour of grief.

The candlestick of the one alone flickers silver in the
    darkening room,
Dying away, when a darkness thinks of the other
And the stone head bends over something ephemeral,

Drunk from wine and sweet night melodies.
Ever the ear follows
The soft lament of the blackbird in the hazel bush.

Dark hour of the rosary. Who are you?
Lone flute,
Forehead, freezing, bending over black times.

In the Winter

When snow falls at the window,
The evening bells toll a long time,
The table is set for many
And the house well appointed.

Some few of them on the road
Come to the gate up dark pathways.
Full of mercy his wounds are dressed
By the gentle strength of love.

O! Man's naked agony.
Who wrestled with angels speechless,
Reaches bested by holy pain
Silent for God's bread and wine.

Nightly Lament

The night has risen over the tousled brow
With beautiful stars
Over the face petrified with pain,
A wild beast devoured the lover's heart
A fiery angel
Falls on a stony field with an agonized breast,
A vulture flaps upwards once more.
Woe in an endless lament
Fire mingles, earth and a blue spring

Passion

When Orpheus strums the lute silver,
Lamenting one dead in the evening garden—
Who are you one reposed under towering trees?
The autumn reeds rustle the lament,
The blue pond.

Woe unto the slender body of the boy,
Which glows crimson,
Of a bereaved mother in a blue mantle
Cloaking her holy degradation.

Woe unto one born, that he would die,
Before he relished the burning red fruit,
The bitter of guilt.

For whom do you weep under trees in twilight?
The sister, dark lover
Of a wild breed,
For whom the day rushes by on golden spokes.

O, that night would come more pious,
Christ.

A corpse you search amid greening trees
For your bride,
The silver rose
Drifting over the hill at night.
Walking on the black shore
Of death,
The hell flower blooms crimson in the heart.

Leaning over the sighing water
See your spouse: a face staring from leprosy
And her hair flutters wild in the night.

Two wolves in the dark forest
We mixed our blood in a stone hard embrace
And the stars of our kind fell upon us.

O, the sting of death.
We see ourselves faded on the crossroad
And in silver eyes
The black shadows mirror our wilderness,
A dreadful laughter that cracks apart our mouths.

Thorny steps sink into the dark,
That red of cold feet
The blood streams down upon the stony field.

In a crimson flood
The silver sleeper tosses herself awake.

But that other one became a snowy tree
On a hill of bones,
A wild deer peering from a festering wound,
A silent stone again.

O, the peaceful hour of stars,
Of this crystal sleep,
There in the thorned chamber
The leprous face fell from you.

The soul sounds of lonely strumming,
A dark rapture
Full at the silver feet of her the penitent
In the blue stillness
And expiation of the olive trees[.]

To Johanna

I often hear your footsteps
Tolling through the street.
In the brown garden
The blueness of your shadow.

In the darkening arbour
I sat silent with my wine.
A trickle of blood
Dropped from your temple

Into the singing glass,
The hour of endless despair.
There blows from the stars
A snowy wind through the leaves.

Every kind of death suffers,
The night the pale man.
Your crimson-red mouth
Dwells as a wound within me.

As though I came from the green
Fir hills and the stories told

About our home place,
Which we have long forgotten—

Who are we? A blue lament
Of a mossy forest brook.
Where the violets
Smell secretive in spring.

A peaceful village in summer
Once guarded the childhood
Of our kind,
White descendants dying off

Now on the hill of evening[.]
We dream of the horror
Of our nighted blood[,]
Shadows in a stone city.

Evening Land

Else Lasker-Schüler—in adoration

1

Ruined hamlets mired
In the brown November,
The dark paths of the villagers
Among deformed dwarf-
Apple trees, the laments
Of the women in silver crape.

The fathers' line withers away.
The evening wind fills
With sighs
For the ghost of the forests.

In silence the footbridge leads
To cloudlike roses
A tame deer on the hill
And in the dark
The blue brooks sound,
Such that a softness
A child will be born.

Silently at the crossroads
The shadow parted from the stranger
And the watching eyes
Become stone blind,
Such that from the lips
The song flows sweeter;

For it is night
The abode of the lover,
The blue face is speechless
Over something dead,
The temple gaping;
A crystal scene;

Which is followed on dark paths
Along walls
By someone who is dead.

2

When it has become night
Our stars appear in the sky
Among ancient olive trees,
Or along dark cypresses
We wander white roads;
A sword-bearing angel:
My brother.
The mouth turned stone silences
The dark song of pain.

Once more a corpse responds
In white linen
And a great many blossoms
Fall across the rock path.

Something sick weeps silver,
Leprous by the pond,
Where ages ago
Lovers rested joyful in the afternoon.

Or the steps sound
Of Elis through the grove,
The hyacinthine,
Once more to fade among oaks.
O the boy's figure
Formed from crystal tears
And shadows in the night.

Or else the brow discerns perfect things,
The chill, childlike,
When over greening hills
A spring storm sounds.

3

So quiet are the green forests
Of our home[.]
The sun sets on the hill
And we have wept in sleep;

Wander with white footsteps
Along the thorny hedge[,]
Those singing in the wheat-eared summer
And those bearing pain.

Already the grain ripens for mankind,
The sacred vine.
And in a stone room,
In its coolness, the meal is prepared.
Also the heart
Of the good is soothed in green stillness
And the cool of tall trees.
He dishes out the food with soft hands.

Manifold is a thing waxing
In the starry night
And beautiful the blue,
A whiteness striding, a breathing thing,
A plucking of strings.

The brother reclined on the hill
And a stranger,
One abandoned by people, him lowering
His moist eyelids
In unspeakable melancholy.
From black clouds
Trickle bitter poppies.

The path falls moon-white silent
Alongside these poplars
And soon
Mankind's wandering ends,
A just indulgence.
Too the stillness of children rejoices,
The nearness of angels
On a crystal meadow.

4

A boy with a shattered breast
Dies away a song in the night.
Allow only walking in silence on the hill
Under the trees
Followed by the shadow of a deer.
The violets in the meadow smell sweet.

Or allow entering the stone house,
Lowering the head
In the shadow of the grief-stricken mother.
In wet blueness a small lamp lights
The nightlong;
For the pain no longer sleeps;

Too are the white shapes
Of those breathing, friends who went far away;
The walls around keep a vast silence.

5

When the street turns dark
And something long dead
Responds in blue linen,
O, how the echoing footsteps reel
And the greening head keeps silent.

Cities are built up
And from stone in the plain;
But the homeless follows
With an open brow to the wind,
To the trees on the hill;
Too the red sunset often casts fear.

Soon the waters rush
Loud in the night,
The angel touches
A girl's crystal cheeks,
Her blond hair,
Weighed down by the sister's tears.

Often this is love: The stranger's
Cold fingers are touched
By a blossoming thorn bush
In passing;
And the cottages of the villagers fade
Into the blue night.

In a childlike stillness,
In the grain, where speechless a cross looms,
To the onlooker there appears
Sighing his shadow and passage.

Melancholy

The blue soul has withdrawn itself in silence,
Brown woods recede in the open window,
The stillness of dark beasts; in the valley
The mill grinds, clouds rest pouring down the footbridge,

The golden stranger. A team of horses leaps red
In the village. The garden brown and cold.
Asters freeze, by the fence painted so thin
The sunflower's gold has nearly all dispersed.

The voices of young girls calling; dew is spilt
Into the hard grass and stars white and cold.
Painted into the dear shadow see death,
Each face full of tears and withdrawn to themselves.

To Lucifer

Lend to this ghost your flames, a glowing despair;
His head looms up sighing into midnight,
On the greening hill of the spring; where before time
A gentle lamb was bled, which endured the deepest
Pain; but the Dark One follows the shadow
Of evil, or he raises up his wet pinions
To the golden disc of the sun and there rips
A sound of bells through that pain-torn breast of his,
Wild hope; the eclipse of a flaming downfall.

[*Take, blue evening, one's temple, of one who slumbers*]

Take, blue evening, one's temple, of one who slumbers
Quietly beneath autumnal trees, beneath a golden cloud.
The forest watches; while the boy a blue deer dwelt
In the crystal ripples of the cold stream,
Thus his heart beat quietly in the hyacinthine twilight,
The shadow of his sister mourns, her crimson hair;
That gutters in the night wind. The other one
Sleepwalks sunken paths and his red mouth dreams
Beneath the rotting trees; the coldness of the pond
Surrounds the sleeper in silence, across
His blackish eyes the fallen moon glides.
Stars engulfed in the brown oak limbs.

In the Evening

The grass is still yellow, the forest grey and black;
But a green dawns in the evening.
The river comes from the mountains cold and clear,
Sounds in the rock den; thus it sounds
When you exercise your legs intoxicated; a wild walk
In the blue, and the ecstatic calls of the birds.
The one already very dark, the forehead
Lowers over bluish water, something which is female;
Going under once more in a green branch of the evening.
Footsteps and melancholy sound as one in a crimson sun.

Over New Wine

The sun is going down crimson,
A swallow has flown very far.
Beneath the archways of evening,
New wine goes round the circle;
Snow falls past the mountain.

Summer's last green blows away,
A hunter comes drawn from the woods.
Beneath the archways of evening,
New wine goes round the circle;
Snow falls past the mountain.

A bat flies around the brow,
A stranger comes drawn in silence.
Beneath the archways of evening,
New wine goes round the circle;
Snow falls past the mountain.

[*Gloom*]

In inns often dreaming the afternoon,
In gardens soon by autumn seared and bare,
Drunken Death walks past in silence and nods[.]
A thrush call sounds from inside a dark cage.

Out of such blueness a pink child appears
And he plays with his eyes black and shining.
Something gold drips from branches meek and mild[.]
But the wind is playing in the red leaves.

How Saturn glows. In the dark the stream roars
And quietly the friend's blue hand rises
And calmly smoothens his forehead and robe.
A light wakes shadows in the elder trees.

[The night swallowed red faces]

The night swallowed red faces,
Along a wall of hair
A childlike skeleton gropes in the shadow
Of the drunkard, a broken smile
In the wine, a burning despair,
Mental torture—a stone silences
The blue voice of the angel
In the ear of the sleeper. Fallen light.

On

These brown roof beams have ·
The coolness of dark years, pain and hope
Over which dahlias hang in flames.
As though a golden helmet fell from a bloody forehead
The day ends in stillness,
Childhood softly looks on from blackish eyes.
Quietly the red beeches shine forth in the evening,
Love, hope, such that from blue lids
Dew drips unstoppably.
Lonely homecoming! The dark calls of the fisherman
Ever echo on the darkening river;
Love, night, the despair's crystal minutes
Shimmering away, stars, already looking on more still[.]

Homecoming

When the evening breathes golden peace,
There before the forest and dark meadow
Man is one watching,
A shepherd, dwelling in the flocks' darkening stillness,
The patience of the red beeches;
Here autumn becomes so clear. On the hill
The one alone listens to the flight of birds,
A dark meaning and the shadows of the dead
Have gathered around him more earnest[;]
The cool scent of mignonettes fills him with shivering[,]
The cottages of the villagers[,] the elderberry,
Where long ago the child dwelt.

These brown roof beams have
Memory, buried hope
Over which dahlias hang,
Such that he wrings his hands for them,
In the brown garden the shimmering footsteps
Of forbidden love, a dark year,
Such that tears fell unstoppably
From the blue eyelids of the stranger.

The dew drips from brown treetops,
As this other awakes a blue deer on the hill,
Listening to the loud calls of the fishermen
By the pond of evening,
To the ill-favoured cries of the bats;
But in golden stillness
Dwells the drunken heart
Full of its sublime death.

Autumn Homecoming

These brown roof beams have
Memory, buried hope
Over which dahlias hang,
An ever-stiller homecoming,
The fallen garden a dark echo
Of childhood years,
Such that tears fall from blue eyelids
Unstoppably;
The despair's crystal minutes
Shimmer away
Into night.

Reverie

Lovers walk by hedgerows,
Which are filled with fragrances.
With evening joyful guests come
From the darkening street.

Pensive chestnuts in the inn-house garden.
The wet bells become silent.
A boy sings by the river
—fire, which seeks a thing of darkness—

O blue stillness! Patience!
When everything blossoms!

Night grant gentle courage
To the homeless as well,
Unfathomable darkness,
A golden hour in wine.

Psalm

Stillness; as the blind sank along an autumnal wall,
Listening with rotted temples to the flight of ravens;
Autumn's golden stillness, the face of the father in guttering
    sunlight
With evening the old village falls in the peace of brown oaks,
The red hammering of the blacksmith, a beating heart.
Stillness; in slow hands the maidservant buries her
    hyacinthine brow
Among fluttering sunflowers. Fear and silence
The darkening room fills bursting eyes, the hesitant footsteps
Of old women, the flight of the crimson mouth, which
    slowly burns out in the darkness.

Silent evening in wine. From the low rafters
Fell a night moth, a nymph buried in blue sleep.
In the yard the servant slaughters a lamb, the sweet smell of
    the blood
Clouds our foreheads, the dark coolness of the well.
The despair mourns dying asters, a golden voice in the wind.
When night falls you will look at me with mouldering eyes,
In blue stillness your cheeks fell into dust.

A weed fire dies out so quietly, the black hamlet falls
        silent in the valley
As the cross descended Mount Calvary's blue hill,
The silent earth expels its dead.

Sight

Autumn so red and quiet here
Under elms of dark torment[,]
Twilit village and love-feast[.]
A falcon waves in golden flight.

A forehead bleeds softly and dark[.]
Sunflowers wilt by the fence[.]
In women's fold despair blues;
The word of God in the starlight!

Crimson flickers a mouth and lie.
Cold in a fallen bedroom,
Just laughter shines, golden play,
Such that a storm would dash this head

Nightly with lightning; blackly falls
Foul fruit from the tree at night.
A child at your blue tassel[,]
I have to pass by in silence.

To the Night

Nymph pull me into your darkness;
Asters freeze and shake by the fence,
In women's fold despair blues;
Bleeding crucifix in starlight.

Crushed crimson a mouth and lie
Cold in a fallen chamber;
Yet laughter shines, golden play;
A bell during the final pulls.

A cloud of blue! Blackly there falls
Thudding rotten fruit from the tree
And the room becomes the grave
And dull earthly pilgrimage dream.

Dwindlings

O ghostly reunion
In the old autumn.
Yellow roses
Shed leaves by the garden fence,
An enormous pain dissolved
In a dark tear,
O sister!
So still ends the golden day.

[*Sleep*]

Take courage, you dark poisons
Producing white sleep
A most peculiar garden
Of darkening trees
Filled with serpents, moths,
Bats;
Stranger your woeful shadow
Staggers, bitter tribulation
In the red sunset!
Age-old isolated waters
Seeped into the sand.

White hart at night's edge
Stars perhaps!
Veiled in spider's web
Shimmers dead spittle.
An iron look.
Thorns float around
The blue path into the village
A crimson laughter
To the eavesdropper in an empty tavern.
Across the threshing floor
Dances moon-white
The evil's enormous shadow.

Stages of Life

Ghostlier burns the wild
Roses at the garden fence;
O silent soul!

In the cool grape leaves feeds
The crystal sun;
O holy purity!

An old man holds out with noble
Hands ripened fruit.
O look of love!

The Sunflowers

You golden sunflowers,
Devoutly bowed in dying,
You meekful sisters
In such stillness
Helian's year ends
Of mountainous cold.

Here his drunken brow
Pales from kisses
Amid those golden
Flowers of despair[.]
The silent darkness
Affects the ghost.

[*So grave O summer twilight*]

So grave O summer twilight.
From a tired mouth
Your golden breath sank into the valley[,]
Into those havens of shepherds,
Sinks in the leaves.
A vulture at the forest's edge
Lifts the stone-changed head—
An eagle's glance
Shines in the grey clouds
Of night.

Wild glow
The red roses by the fence[,]
Something loving
Dies glowing away in a green wave
A faded rose[.]

Published Prose and Poetry, 1913–1915

After a month-long journey through all of Galicia, heartfelt greetings. For several days I was quite sick from unspeakable grief, I believe. Today I am glad, for we will almost surely be marching north and, in a few days perhaps, already be back in Russia. Heartfelt greetings to Herr Kraus.

Georg Trakl to Alfred Loos, early October 1914

He is surely no victim of war. It was always inconceivable to me that he could live. His madness wrestled with godly things.

Karl Kraus to Sidonie Nädherny von Borutin, November 1914

There is one other poem in Grete Trakl's distinctively large and flowing hand, which resembles musical notation and differs markedly from her brother's crabbed and seemingly unreadable script. 'Helian's Song of Destiny' ('Helians Schicksalslied') is provisionally attributed to Grete's authorship, composed when she was a guest of von Ficker in December 1914 and early January 1915, when she was given some of the money and possessions left to her by her late brother.

The title echoes Hölderlin's poem 'Hyperion's Song of Destiny', a paean to the Greek concept of the tragic fall. For those who would read incest into the poem, its three quatrains (see the note on p. 265) would seem to be Grete's confession. Describing a day of nuptials, 'full of joy', of 'stepping through the drunken grove', of celebrating 'our high time' (from the German *hohe Zeit*, or wedding), it could almost be a passionate reprise of the Gnostic spiritual marriage between Christ and Mary Magdalene in Trakl's eponymous prose piece from *A Golden Chalice*. The poem ends, too, as though it were a suicide pact, with the sublimated death of Helian and his bride, who 'blaze from dawn to dawn's red sunrise'.

A year earlier, in January 1914, Trakl had spoken of Christ and sex in a conversation—recorded by an observer—with the writer Carl Dallago, another contributor to the *Brenner* circle, shortly after a series of lectures by Karl Kraus in Innsbruck. Kraus, as always, incited much discussion and undoubtedly Dallago must have wanted to get the famously reserved Trakl to speak on some controversial subject. The latter however is not the real *provocateur*.

Dallago began by prodding Trakl to give an opinion on Walt Whitman, who was much read and admired in Central Europe during this time. Such a question seemed fair, for Trakl now wrote in free verse. Surprisingly, he found the American poet 'perverse'. Then the conversation turned to how Trakl and Whitman stood in contrast to each other. Whitman celebrated life in all its varied forms while Trakl was thoroughly the pessimist. Dallago picked up on this and goaded Trakl further, asking him why he found 'no joy in life' and whether his work gave him 'any satisfaction at all'.

'But,' Trakl replied, 'one must mistrust that satisfaction.'

Dallago leant back in his chair in utter astonishment. Then, after a brief silence, he asked, 'So why don't you just enter a monastery?'

'I am Protestant,' Trakl answered.

'Pro . . . te . . . stant?' asked Dallago. 'I would have never thought such a thing!'

Taking Trakl for some kind of monk, Dallago suggested he leave the hustle and bustle of city life for the country.

'I have no right to deprive myself of hell,' responded Trakl.

'But even Christ withdrew himself,' said Dallago.

'Christ is God's son,' answered Trakl.

Dallago, an anti-clericalist, could hardly contain himself and pressed on with what had now become a spiritual disputation. 'So, you also must believe that all salvation comes from him. You do understand "God's son" in the strict sense of the word?'

'I am Christian,' said Trakl.

'Indeed,' continued Dallago, 'then how do you explain such unchristian manifestations as Buddha or the Chinese philosophers?'

'They receive their light from Christ, too.'

Everyone present was left speechless, contemplating the depth of his paradox. Dallago, however, would not let it go. 'And the Greeks? Don't you believe too that humankind has sunk much lower since then?'

'Never has mankind sunk lower since the appearance of Christ,' retorted Trakl. 'It could never sink so low!' he added after a short pause.

Then Dallago produced his last trump card: 'Nietzsche?'

'Nietzsche was insane!' Trakl replied, his eyes flashing.

'How do you mean that?'

'I mean that Nietzsche had the same disease as Maupassant!'

Trakl's face looked monstrous as he said this—meaning syphilis—and his eyes burnt as though he were possessed by 'the Demon of Lies'. To this Dallago responded with such strength and moral authority that no one else could have responded in kind: 'You must know that insanity has mental causes!'

Trakl, who had lowered his head, looked up and sized up his opponent with a strange, silent stare. Then, after a while, he seemed to reflect on what he said about Christ and Nietzsche, the unbeliever to whom so many of Trakl's contemporaries ascribed. 'It is uncanny how Christ with each simple word resolves the deepest question of humankind! You can totally resolve the question of communion between man and woman through the command: They shall become one flesh.' With that shocking shift—like those in his poems—in emphasis, the conversation turned to a subject that would almost seem *less* controversial—Dostoevsky and the noble prostitute Sonia in *Crime and Punishment*, a character Trakl considered a moral emblem. But what did he mean by a pronouncement, which even made free love a sacrament? It could excuse incest, too. It could allude to some philosophical and aesthetic form of androgyny, which he and his lookalike sister evinced. It would explain what he meant by 'One kind' in the poem 'Evening Land Song'.

The time leading up to Trakl's testament of faith and living in *imitatio Christi*—the second half of 1913—had been marked by bouts of depression and panic attacks. By the end of the year, von Ficker described his friend's condition as like someone dead, a 'surreal theatre'—suggesting both its intensity as well as the possibility that it seemed to be a kind of performance for onlookers. Nevertheless, von Ficker and his wife Cäcilie were supportive and gave Trakl a place to visit, to dine, to meet friends, willing ears to hear him or wait out his long silences. But they could do little but marvel at his voracious appetite for alcohol and 'habit drugs'. (Trakl did seek professional treatment for his depression. What his doctor and neurologist gave him—Veronal—was seen as effective for overcoming the cravings for cocaine and morphine as well as their withdrawal symptoms.)

Children, too, had a good effect on Trakl, and surely for this reason he enjoyed being in the company of von Ficker's young family. And, despite his dark moods, Trakl could be an easy travelling companion, as he was in the summer of 1913, when he accompanied the von Fickers on a vacation to Venice and the Lido in a party that included Adolf and Bessie Loos, Karl Kraus and Peter Altenberg. During the coming months, Trakl gave his first (and only) public reading in Innsbruck. But while his audience saw a new entertainment under the catchall of Expressionism, Trakl saw himself as a lost and doomed soul, a self-aware Kaspar Hauser and an increasingly hermetic and isolated figure, like the tonsured monk which he drew, a self-portrait intended to be satirical, self-deprecatory. And yet Trakl really was a rising figure in German poetry as he began to publish outside *Die Brenner* in prominent venues such as the Christmas issue of the *Reichspost*, Vienna's conservative newspaper. But again, he did not see himself rising, just falling, going down. Fortunately, his friends and supporters saw the best in him while he existed seemingly from one poem to the other and without 'literary ambition' as they understood. To them, perhaps, Trakl was a pure artist and only the care he took in his work saved him from his mounting despair during the winter of 1913–14.

The reason for that despair has been the subject of much scholarship. One theory is Trakl's knowledge that his sister was pregnant. His letters, poems, behaviour and talk during this time have been interpreted as encoded confessions of his paternity, and his fear of having to deal with the inevitable proof of an incestuous relationship with Grete. But there is no evidence of any face-to-face contact between them throughout 1913. Indeed, the only evidence that exists suggests a distancing, a silence between the two, perhaps even avoidance (so that nothing could happen between them). Thus, any child of Georg and Grete had to be the result of an immaculate incest. Still, Trakl spent much of January and February 1914 drunk and despondent, and he surely obsessed over his sister's welfare.

In March, Trakl pulled himself together for two reasons. He signed a contract with Kurt Wolff for a new book of poems, to be titled *Sebastian Dreaming*. Such an endeavor which would require much energy, diligence and self-possession on his part. He also learned that Grete needed him in Berlin. When he arrived, he discovered his sister bedridden and alone in her small apartment. She had suffered what Trakl termed a *Fehlgeburt*, a 'miscarriage' or 'stillbirth'; but the same word is an euphemism for an abortion. Legally, if there had been a child, it would be Langen's. His presence during this time goes unmentioned by Trakl—suggesting that Grete's pregnancy was not her husband's affair, either by his choice or his wife's.

The case made for Trakl's paternity is his poetry and his strange, even guilty behaviour and pronouncements during the winter of 1913–14. But Trakl had long been absent from Grete's life. Albeit a self-styled vagabond, he did not stray in the direction of Berlin, given his extant correspondence. If he had met Grete in Salzburg, and in a way to accommodate the timetable for human conception and gestation, there is no puzzle piece for that—just what one chooses to decrypt from poems and a poet's madness.

There is, too, no way of knowing when Trakl learned of his sister's pregnancy—but he, perhaps more than her own husband, would have been the one most sympathetic to her plight. If she were to die, Georg would be the one she would most want to be by her. He is also the one who had some medical training, even though dispensing drugs in garrison hospitals was hardly what was needed for a woman seemingly bleeding out like a wounded soldier on the battlefield. And if he witnessed the course of the miscarriage and its insult to his sister's body, he was hardly a midwife or one who could perform or assist in a surgical abortion. Yet Trakl, the pharmacist, could have helped his sister with an induced miscarriage, which entailed not only moral guilt, but civil too, a form of homicide under German and Austrian law at the time. Such speculation provides a logical puzzle piece given certain poems, with their fragmented images of fallow procreation and dead lines of descent. Such a piece would help to explain such poems and the reason for Trakl's winter–spring despair. But it would have to be forced into an eternally incomplete picture with both thumbs now or sit somewhere alone in the middle.

After Trakl had Grete stable, he wrote a few friends in Innsbruck about her 'alarming' condition—she had lost a lot of blood and had not eaten in five days. 'My poor sister is still very sick,' he noted in his letter to von Ficker. 'Her life is one of heart-rending sadness and, at the same time, plain courage, which at times makes me feel small in the face of it; and she would a thousand times more worthy to live surrounded by good and fine people, as was granted to me in difficult times to such an overwhelming degree.' He continued, informing that he would stay with his sister for a few more days since she was 'all alone and my presence is of some benefit for her'.

Gradually, however, he found time to leave Grete's bedside. His most memorable encounter was with Else Lasker-Schüler, a friend and correspondent of von Ficker and a poet whose work the editor championed as much as Trakl's. In what little time they spent together, he apparently fell instantly—and platonically—in love with the older woman—as she did with him.

In the spring of 1914, Trakl looked forward to bringing Grete to Innsbruck so that she might benefit from the fine weather and mountain air. But von Ficker's wife fell ill, making it impossible for him to host the poet's sister. In late May, an article appeared in the Vienna *Neue Freie Presse* in which Trakl was included among profiles of Stefan George, Rainer Maria Rilke and Franz Werfel. In July, the philosopher Ludwig Wittgenstein gave von Ficker 100,000 crowns to award to any 'impecunious' writer he liked. From that largesse, Trakl received the most, an honorarium of 20,000 crowns, worth $95,000 at this writing. And Wittgenstein was pleased by the choice, although he confessed that he 'did not understand' Trakl's poems though they had a 'pleasing tone', the 'tone of a truly brilliant person'. (The admission is all the more incredible, for Wittgenstein, the author of the *Tractatus Logico-philosophicus*, sets forth in mathematically precise terms the limitations of language in relating reality.)

Trakl had little opportunity to enjoy his newfound wealth as he began to finalize *Sebastian Dreaming*. In late June, the heir to the Austro-Hungarian throne, Archduke Franz Ferdinand, was assassinated. In a matter of weeks, what would become the First World War began to unfold and Trakl was mobilized; but rather than being assigned to a field hospital, he was deployed with a frontline infantry unit as one of its medics. In August, he found himself on a troop train heading east for Galicia, where the Austrian high command intended to invade the Russian half of that Polish region.

During the early days of September, Trakl's regiment, part of the Fourth Army, encountered the Russians near the town of Grodek. The engagement, known as the Battle of Rawa-Ruska, resulted in enormous casualties. Trakl, whose role was still that of a pharmacist, was put in charge of caring for ninety wounded with nothing but a commandeered barn for a field hospital and scant drugs or training to deal with the carnage. As he tried to relieve the pain of the suffering, amid their cries of pain, he heard, as he told von Ficker later, a 'weak detonation' and saw that a soldier had killed himself with a gunshot wound to the head. Disturbed by the sight of blood and brains splattered against the barn wall, Trakl ran away from his charges into a wooded area where he witnessed another horror: the corpses of Ukrainian peasants dangling eerily from the trees—all hanged.

In the six weeks that followed, Trakl's regiment retreated westwards uneventfully and slowly. His letters during this time seem almost cheerful, if not resigned, to the war and soberly reflective and observant, even though one doctor who examined him noted that Trakl had been using 'large amounts of cocaine' for some time. To von Ficker he wrote of the arduous march further west, 'morning after morning'. While camped in the small town of Limanowa, he described the 'gentle and serene' hills that surrounded him and that the atmosphere reminded him of the recent peace. However, despite the warm autumn weather and the stark beauty of the farmland and rural villages, Trakl feared what he saw as preparations for 'a new great battle' or 'slaughter'. Soon after, he told his fellow soldiers he intended to shoot himself with his service pistol. They disarmed him and he was committed to a military hospital in Krakow on 6 October—which, he was told, was a reassignment. But instead of dispensing drugs to the patients, he was put in an observation cell.

Although depressed and probably sedated, Trakl tended to his poetry. He also wrote friends of his whereabouts. During the last two weeks of October, he saw von Ficker and told him about the horrors of Grodek.

On 25 October, Trakl sent a telegram to Kurt Wolff, requesting finished copies of *Sebastian Dreaming*. Wolff, however, could hardly do so as he explained in his response written during the following week. He and his editorial staff had been mobilized and now served in the German army on the Western front. He told Trakl that he would have to wait for the end of the war to see his new book, a matter of a few months according to the publisher.

Trakl likely did not see the letter in which Wolff expressed such optimism among the cards and letters he received in the coming days, including Else Lasker-Schüler's note, which came with a box of chocolate. Trakl also agreed to meet with Ludwig Wittgenstein, who would arrive on 4 November. However, the philosopher arrived too late—Trakl had been found dead in his room on the morning of the previous day. The official medical report termed it 'Suicide from cocaine poisoning!' (the attending physician's exclamation point). In what form remains a mystery. Tablets were used to make solutions. The powdered form, used as a local anaesthetic for nose and throat surgery, could be inhaled. A mystery too is how Trakl obtained enough of the drug. As an officer, he had an orderly named Matthias Roth assigned to serve him as a *Bursche* (a 'gofer' in Austrian military parlance). Thus, through Roth, Trakl could have procured all the cocaine he needed—but it would not have been the drug of choice for suicide. Indeed, cocaine was seen as alternative–antidote to opiates and alcohol, both of which would be ill suited for a soldier and a poet who wanted to desperately see his new book published and who was producing new poems, war poems unlike any other.

Trakl had sent these to von Ficker for commentary and future publication during his last days and, in that, there would seem to be a will to live. The only thing that would suggest otherwise was the correspondence that accompanied the new work, which included his last poem, 'Grodek'. In one of these letters from the last days of October, Trakl asked the editor if he would oversee his 'wish and intention' that Grete receive all the money he had left from of Wittgenstein's 20,000 crowns, which he had barely touched, and his property—meaning, his advance payment for *Sebastian Dreaming*. His act seemed in keeping with the watch- words he had written before joining his regiment in August: 'Understanding during moments of a corpselike existence: All people are worthy of love. Awakening you feel the bitterness of the world; therein is all your open debt; your poem a partial atonement.'

As dire as it might seem to give away his money and possessions to his sister, Trakl wrote Wittgenstein five or six days later, informing his benefactor that he very much looked forward to his visit in the coming days. Trakl wrote, too, that he expected to be released in a matter of days and 'sent back into the field'.

Then there is the tale Roth wrote von Ficker later which adds further doubt to Trakl's death being a suicide. The orderly had been with Trakl the evening before he died, which would have been Sunday, 1 November, All Souls' Day. Roth had grown fond of Trakl, who, hardly the product of an Austrian military school and hardly a martinet, spoke to the former miner in a soft and 'brotherly' manner. Trakl only requested that Roth bring him a *Schwarzen* (a cup of black coffee) the next day, Monday, 2 November. However, Roth had not been allowed to enter Trakl's room for a twenty-four-hour period as Trakl lay dying. That he could do nothing for Trakl bothered Roth, but he did serve as the only mourner at service held before the hurried burial. Whether Roth was suspicious or simply loyal to his officer, he requested that the coffin be opened before it was interred in a

Krakow cemetery. As he examined the poet's corpse, he noticed an incision, shaped like a half-moon, on the left temple. A shape—that strangely resonates with images from Trakl's poems, suggesting that an autopsy had been performed or some psychosurgical precursor to the lobotomy procedures of the 1940s. If so, the intervention had gone wrong.

Naturally, von Ficker was left to wonder what really happened to his friend. He had his suspicions too. But, as Karl Kraus believed, it seemed incredible that Trakl had lived as long as he did, constantly telegraphing his death and taking risks with his life every time he took drugs. Von Ficker had to wonder, too, given the last time he saw Trakl, when the latter opened a book by the German Baroque poet Johann Christian Günther and read the poem, 'Bußgedanken' (Penitential Thoughts). Von Ficker, ever patient with his friend, had listened carefully to Trakl's quiet and haunting voice, his unpretentious monotony as it set up the closure, the verse that Günther's wanted written on his coffin—'Oft is a good death the best curriculum vitae'—before he too died at the age of twenty-seven.

That Trakl treated his heir Grete as generously as a widow is not only illustrative of his love for his sister but also the faith he had in her, that she be a continuation rather than a sad coda to his own tragic end. He had to know she needed the money, that her marriage to her impecunious husband was unhappy—and that Grete, perhaps like him, was living proof that their *generation*, their *kind* was a dead end as he saw in his poems. Trakl may have seen her as owning them as well. Although the concept of intellectual property did not exist as we know it today, the words he chose for von Ficker did not exclude her possession of his papers. But it was likely understood by all parties that Trakl's long-time editor and friend knew best, which did not exclude Grete from being Georg's champion, his flame-keeper. This role Grete assumed after her brother's death ended the distance he had placed between her and his work.

Trakl probably told Grete nothing of what he experienced at Grodek, his suicide attempt in the field or his hospitalization. She still believed her brother was alive on 6 November. On that day, Langen wrote von Ficker to inform him that Grete had read his most recent letter in which he, von Ficker, had described her brother's condition. However, according to Langen, the news left Grete 'sick and miserable', such that she required a doctor (not to mention the inconvenience of his fee) who requested that she receive no more news of her brother unless it was good.

It was during this time that Else Lasker-Schüler, being one of the first in Berlin to know that Trakl had died, felt obligated to comfort Grete. It had to be done despite the awkward circumstances of her first encounter with Grete the year before, when Else honoured Trakl's written request that she visit his 'poor sister' in his place. When Else did so, in the company of Georg Meyer, Kurt Wolff's agent in Berlin, she found Grete to be brusque with her, such that 'Frau Langen' had 'shown her the door' while making all kinds of false excuses. Else, however, did not hold this against the other woman and her sympathy for Grete must have grown after meeting her brother in person, first in March and then in October. Else had even planned to visit Trakl on the day of his death, when she had a vision of him walking through her room as a young man of fifteen dressed in a Havelock cape, with the collar turned up.

While this vision may have been a later embellishment, Else certainly had real news of Trakl's death before his sister. When she attempted to offer Grete her condolences and a bouquet in person, she realized Grete had no knowledge of her brother's passing and could not handle the real reason for the flowers. After a week passed, Georg Meyer broke the news on his own—and Else returned to comfort Grete and even spent an evening with her, which was civil and pleasant given the circumstances. That Trakl's body was now buried in a strange land was one thing that distressed Grete. She wanted her brother's remains returned to Salzburg—but she needed money. Seeing an opportunity to help Trakl's sister, Else wrote von Ficker, urging him to withdraw 160 marks from the advance paid by Wolff for *Sebastian Dreaming*. 'I would never,' Else wrote, 'leave a friend in the lurch.'

Else's intercession proved to be the path to hell in a matter of days in the wake of Trakl's death. The next time she met Grete, the latter's resentments were no longer filtered by grief. Grete badmouthed Langen—presumably absent once more. To others in their circle, Grete turned her rage on the Jews. Grete even sent Else a letter in which she stated that 'every Jew must be shipped off to Asia'—a remark Else found particularly cruel given that thousands of Jews, many of the fine artists, were shedding their blood for Germany and Austria. Another incident soon followed in a cafe where Grete, drinking heavily, confronted a composer who wanted to use Else's poems for songs and berated him and Jews once more.

Else then responded with a strongly worded letter of her own. Although lost, it may have had some of the flavour that she used to describe the Langens to von Ficker, calling Grete out on her anti-Semitism, her petty-bourgeois envy and, worst of all, her being a 'copy of her friend'—Trakl—and Grete's boozing (*Sauferei*) as 'emulation'. Grete, to Else, was simply this 'banal philosophical romantic' worthy of a trite novel and the false indignation of her husband's insults, for what hurt Else most was his letter ordering her to stop corresponding with his wife and that he had spoken to von Ficker about Else. This last straw prompted Else to enclose his letter and tell of the whole affair. 'This woman,' Else wrote, 'spoke nothing but malice to me, she pursued me with jealousy. I have never suffered such antipathy and I went and called on her for Georg.'

Else was a proud woman with an imposing, even theatrical presence and a mind that impressed Georg Trakl. How she held herself is apparent in her letters, illustrated with her flamboyant self-portraits, bobbed hair and jutting chin, signed with the name of her male and self-exalted alter ego, Prince Yusuf of Thebes. All this perhaps intimidated Grete or left her unimpressed—or even suspicious that Else was attempting to appropriate her brother's ghost, what rightfully belonged to her, the sister, the heir apparent. But Grete's outbursts had invited a troubling question that Else posed to von Ficker: 'Did Trakl have such views too about J? I want to know. I am a Jew. Thank God. [. . .] In this way, I the prince thought [. . .]'.*

For a long time, Else was unable to write or think of Trakl. Eventually, however, she did write three poems inspired by him. And Grete carried her brother's flame—or, rather, clung to it herself—in quite another way, more like a *moll*, while doing more

* Von Ficker perhaps knew that their friend may have said uncomfortable things, specifically the whorehouse aphorism Trakl circulated among his friends ('When a Jew fucks, he gets crabs! A Christian hears every angel sing.') added as postscript to a card sent to Buschbeck in November 1911, undersigned together with Kaspar Hauer! But its meaning is ironical and has this blowback. Trakl undoubtedly means the anti-Semitism of Austrian prostitutes, their Jewish clients' anxiety over hygiene and the Christian faith that the gentile client placed in faked orgasms. Had 'Prince Yusuf' known of this remark, she might have been as much in awe of Trakl's very human wit as she was of his verse.

damage to herself. In a photograph taken of her when she stayed with the von Fickers during the Christmas holiday, she appears to wear the black mourning clothes of a widow—not unusual for a female sibling. Her face is puffy, betraying her heavy use of alcohol. She looks reposed, with the von Fickers' dog seemingly quite comfortable in her lap, but the incident with Else surely resulted in self-defence and justification that would hardly contribute to Georg's reputation. Indeed, there would be other like outbursts over the next two and half years. Being Georg Trakl's sister provided Grete with little direction that pointed the way out of her immediate needs and troubles. 'This money burns my fingers,' she wrote her older sister Maria—and their brother was still buried in Krakow. (In the same letter, Grete has the presence of mind to warn her sister not to touch the curare still hidden in Georg's desk in Salzburg.)

But Grete did burn through her money. And she had already burnt out as a concert pianist, giving way to another of Buhlig's students, his other 'Grete', the eight-year-old Jewish child prodigy Johanna Margarete Sultan. In this way, Grete became for Langen an expensive liability. She surely tested the goodwill of her brother's friends, too, the most valuable thing she could have inherited from him. She also misinterpreted von Ficker's help and advice and, perhaps, displayed her own Asperger-like symptoms with her unfiltered intimacy and irony. In their correspondence, Grete, like her brother resorts to various self-deprecations ('simulacrum', 'one possessed') and signs herself as a kind of demon lover suggested in his poetry ('Your succubus ret.'), which could all serve as captions to Trakl's favourite photograph of his sister as a very young woman, with her hair loose and her intense, unsmiling and sidelong expression.

Arthur and Grete Langen divorced in March 1916. Since German law required an act of infidelity, the divorce decree named Richard Buhlig as Grete's paramour. Buhlig, however, was a homosexual and more likely did the merciful thing for his friend and student,* playing an easy role for the court to end what had become a miserable marriage for both husband and wife. But this hardly ended Grete's downfall. Unable to find work as a pianist or French teacher, she contemplated hiring herself out as a domestic servant. She could do nothing for herself, until her mother and half-brother interceded and convinced her to take a 'rest cure' at a private sanatorium in Munich. The expense of such a clinic, however, proved too much for her family and, by 1917, Grete returned to Berlin, where she hoped to meet her brother's friend, Erhard Buschbeck. Instead, she accumulated more debts, lived in cheap hotels and was even picked up by the police for vagrancy.

When Grete turned twenty-six that summer, friends who admired her brother's work intervened. They paid her debts, found an apartment for her and encouraged her with plans to become a French translator once the war ended, for French literature was still considered unpatriotic.

On the evening of 21 September, these same friends gave her a party. For all her problems, Grete must have been good company—certainly a good drinking companion—and she knew her brother's work. And, to them, only she could be the 'sister' in the poems, the one who could unravel the mysteries behind them. Lastly, being with Grete, given her identical twin-like

* Buhlig's American lovers include such protégés as Henry Cowell, John Cage and Harry Partch.

225

resemblance to Trakl, served as well to give the dead poet a living presence.

Grete ended her party early, in a way that imprinted herself on her brother's work and legacy for ever, an act that Grete authored in her own right if what little is known about that last evening is true: she rose up, excused herself saying she wanted to fetch her cigarettes, disappeared into an adjoining room. Seconds later a shot rang out and she was found dead from a bullet to the heart. How she obtained the weapon and aimed it with the precision or 'luck' needed to get past bone is uncertain. Wartime Berlin was awash in guns and her closest siblings were well armed. Her sister Mia's pistol is still displayed in a presentation case in the Trakl House, testifying that many women of this era 'carried and concealed' for their own protection. A Browning semi-automatic is recorded among her brother's effects left at Krakow. Yet another puzzle piece which makes the story better— or better than it is?

A Spring Evening

A bush full of larvae; March evening foehn;
A mad dog runs through a desolate field.
The priest's bell jingles through the brown village;
A leafless tree convulses in black pain.

In the shade of old roofs the corn bleeds;
O sweetness, which stills the sparrows' hunger.
Through the yellowed reeds a deer shyly breaks;
O facing waters alone still and white.

Unspeakable looms the walnut tree's ghost.
The boys' rustic game brings cheer to a friend.
Ruined cottages, battered emotion;
The clouds wander low and balling up black.

In an Old Garden

A mignonette smell fades in the brown green,
Iridescence shivers on the beautiful pool,
The willows stand shrouded in a white veil
Within which butterflies circle madly.

Here the terrace suns itself abandoned,
Goldfish glitter deep within the water's glass,
Occasionally clouds float over the hill,
And slowly the strangers go forth again.

The foliage shines brightly, for young women
Had passed this way during the early morning,
Their laughter remained clinging to the small leaves,
In a golden mist dances a drunken faun.

Evening Reel

Fields of asters brown and blue,
Children play there by the grave vaults,
In the open skies of evening,
Blown into the clear skies,
Seagulls hover silver-grey.
Horns call in the flood meadow.

Inside the old tavern screech
Violins madly out of tune,
In the windows sails a ring dance,
Sails a gaudy merry-go-round,
Furious and drunk on wine.
The night comes inside freezing.

Laughter flutters, blows away,
A lute is strumming mockingly,
Softly a silent garden rue,
A melancholy garden rue
Blows down at the threshold.
Cling-clang! A sickle's reaping.

The candles' glow weaves dreamlike,
Paints this youthful flesh decaying,

Cling-clang! Hear it ring in the fog,
Ring in time with the violins,
And bones dance along naked,
Long does the moon peer inside.

Night Soul

In silence a blue deer came down from black forests,
The soul,
When it was night; a snowy stream over mossy steps.

Blood and weapons clashing of times long ago
Rush into the pine valley.
The moon ever shines in fallen rooms;

Intoxicated by dark poisons, a silver larva
Bowed over the slumber of the shepherds,
A head, which silently forsakes its legends.

O, then the other slowly opens cold hands
Rotting in crimson sleep
And the flowers of winter blossom silver

At the forest's edge, the gloomy paths stream
Into the stone city;
Often the owl calls to those drunk out of black despair.

In Hellbrunn

Once more following the evening's blue lament
By the hill, by the springtime pond—
As the shadows of the long dead drifted over it,
The shades of the church's princes, of noble ladies—
Already their flowers bloom, elegiac violets
In evening soil, the blue spring's
Crystal wave rushes. So ghostly green
The oaks above the forgotten paths of the dead,
The golden clouds above the pond.

The Heart

The wild heart turned white with the forest;
O dark fear
Of death, like the gold
Dead in grey clouds.
November evening.
At the bleak gate of the slaughterhouse stood
A throng of poor women;
In every basket
Fell rotting meat and offal;
Accurst fare.

The evening's blue dove
Brought no conciliation.
A dark trumpet's call
Goes through the elms'
Wet gold leaves,
A tattered flag
Steaming of blood,
Such that in wild despair
A man listens.
O! You brazen times
Buried there in the red sunset.

From the dark hallway stepped
The girl-youth's
Golden figure
Surrounded by pale moons,
Autumnal retinue,

Black firs snapped
In the night storm,
The steep castle.
O heart
Shimmering over in snowy cold.

Sleep

Curse you, dark poisons,
White sleep!
This most peculiar garden
Of darkening trees
Filled with serpents, moths,
Spiders, bats.
Stranger! Your forlorn shadow
In the red sunset,
A gloomy corsair
In the salt sea of tribulation.
White birds flutter upward to the night's edge
Over the collapsing cities
Of steel.

The Thunderstorm

You wild mountains, the eagles'
Lofty grief.
Golden clouds
Steam across stone desolation.
The pines breathe a patient stillness,
The black lambs at the crevasse,
Where the blue suddenly,
Strangely falls silent,
The soft humming of bumblebees.
O green flower—
O silence.

Like a dream the wild brook's
Dark spirits stir the heart,
Gloom,
Which descends upon the gorges!
White voices
Wandering through fearsome atriums,
Broken terraces,
The fathers' enormous wrath, the plaints
Of mothers,
The boy's golden war cry

And the unborn's
Sighing from blind eyes.

O pain, you flaming display
Of the great soul!
Already amid the black melee
Of horses and chariots
A terrifying rose bolt
Flashes in the echoing spruce.
A magnetic chill
Hovers about this proud head,
The red-hot melancholy
Of an angry god.

Fear, you poison serpent,
Black, die in the rocks!
Then the tears plunged
Of wild rivers downwards,
A storm's mercy,
In looming thunder,
Snow-capped peaks echo all around.
Fire
Purifies a riven night.

The Evening

With the dead epic figures
Moon you fill
The silent forests,
Sickle moon—
With the soft embrace
Of lovers,
The shades of fabled times
Ring the crumbling cliffs;
So bluely it shines down
On the city,
Where cold and evil
Dwells a rotting generation,
Preparing a dark future
Of white descendants.
You moon-swallowed shadows
Sighing into the empty crystal
Of the mountain lake.

The Night

You I sing wild fissure,
In the night storm
Of towering mountains;
You grey towers
Overflowing with hellish faces,
Fiery beasts,
Tousled ferns, spruces,
Crystal flowers.
Infinite torment,
Such that you trap God
Gentle spirit,
Sighing in the waterfall,
In tossing pines.

The fires of the people
Blaze golden all around.
On black cliffs
The glowing wind's bride
Plunges deathly drunk,
The blue waves
Of glaciers
And there booms

Enormous the bell in the valley:
Flames, curses
And the dark
Performances of lust,
A head turned stone
Storms heaven.

The Despair

You are an enormous dark mouth
Inside, from autumn clouds
A moulded shape,
Golden evening stillness;
A green darkening mountain river
In the shadow ground
Of broken pines;
A village,
Which piously withers away in brown images.

Then the black horses leap
On a pasture in fog.
You soldiers!
From the hill, where the sun wheels dying
The laughing blood rushes—
Amid oaks
Speechless! O the grumbling despair
Of the army, a steel helmet
Dropped clattering from a crimson brow.

An autumn night comes so cool,
With stars
Above the broken bones of men,
Shines the silent she-monk.

The Homecoming

The chill of dark years,
Pain and hope
Cyclopean rocks enshrine,
Desolate mountains,
The autumn's golden breath,
Evening cloud—
Pureness!

From blue eyes watches
Crystal childhood;
Under dark spruce
Love, hope,
That from burning lids
Dew drips in the stiff grass—
Unstoppable!

O! The golden footbridge there
Collapsing into the snow
Of the crevasse!
The night valley
Breathes blue cold,
Faith, hope!
Greetings you lone graveyard!

Lament

Youth from a crystal mouth
Your golden look sank into the valley;
A wave of woods red and pale
In the black hours of the evening.
Evening whips open such deep wounds!

Fear! Death's dream plaint,
Dead grave and the year
Even watches from tree and deer;
Barren field and fertile soil.
The shepherd calls the frightened flock.

Sister, your blue eyebrows beckon
Quietly during the night.
An organ sighs and hell laughs,
A horror seizes the heart;
Star and angel would like to see.

A mother must fear for the child;
The ore rings red in the shaft,
The lust, tears, pain made of stone,
The dark legends of Titans.
Despair! Eagles lament alone.

Night Surrender

She-monk! close me in your darkness,
You mountain chain cold and blue!
Dark dew is bleeding downwards;
A cross looms steep in the starlight.

Crushed purple a mouth and a lie
Cold in a fallen chamber;
Yet laughter shines, golden play,
A bell during the final pulls.

A lunar cloud! Blackly there falls
At night wild fruit from the tree
And the room becomes the grave
And this earthly pilgrimage dream.

In the East

The wild organs of winter storms
Equals the nation's black rage,
The crimson tide of battle,
Defoliated stars.

With agonized eyebrows, silver arms,
The night beckons dying soldiers.
In the shadows of autumn ash trees
Sigh the ghosts of those smited.

A wilderness of thorns girds the city.
From its bloody stations the moon
Chases women in panic.
Wild wolves burst through the gate.

Lament

Sleep and death, the sombre eagles
Sweep around this head nightlong:
The icy wave of eternity
Would suck under the golden effigy
Of mankind. The crimson body
Is battered on ghastly reefs
And the dark voice laments
Over the sea.
Sister of a tempestuous despair,
Behold a fear-ridden rowboat sinks
Under stars,
The silent face of the night.

Grodek

With evening the autumn woods sound
Of deadly arms, the golden plains
And blue lakes, over which the sun
Trundles hazier; the night envelopes
Dying warriors, the wild lament
Of their shattered jaws.
But silent in the willow-marsh gather
Red clouds, wherein an angry god dwells,
The spilt blood itself, lunar cold;
All roads empty into black corruption.
Beneath the golden limbs of night and stars
The sister's shadow goes to and fro through the still grove,
Hailing the ghosts of heroes, the bloody heads;
And the black pipes of autumn play softly in the reeds.
O prouder sorrow! You brass altars
Today a colossal pain feeds the hot flame of the spirit,
The unborn descendants.

Revelation and Perdition

Strange are the night paths of man. As I went forth sleep-walking in stone rooms and a small, still light burnt in each, a copper candlestick, and as I sank down freezing on the bed, once more her black shadow stood overhead, the stranger, and I silently hid my face in unhurried hands. The hyacinth bloomed blue at the window too and the old prayer pressed on the crimson lips of the breathing, from the eyelids fell crystal tears wept for this bitter world. In this hour during the death of my father, I was the white son. The night wind came from the hill in blue shivers, the dark lament of the mother, dying away again, and I saw the black hell in my heart; a minute of shimmering stillness. Quietly an unspeakable face emerged from a chalk wall—a dying youth—the beauty of some homecoming offspring. Moon-white the coolness of the stone surrounded the vig-ilant temple, the footsteps of the shadow faded on the ruined steps, a pink ring dance in the little garden.

I sat silently in a deserted tavern under wood beams filled with smoke and alone over a glass of wine; a shining corpse bowed over something dark and it laid a dead lamb at my feet. From a festering blue, the pale figure of the sister emerged and spoke her bleeding mouth thus: Prick black thorn. Ah my silver arms still ring of wild thunderstorms. Drip blood from my moon feet, florid on night paths, over which the rat scurries squeaking. Your star flickers in my arched brows; and quietly the heart tolls in the night. A red shadow with a flaming sword broke into the house, fled with a snow-covered forehead. O bitter death.

And from me a dark voice spoke: I broke the neck of my black horse in the night forest when madness sprang from its crimson eyes; the shadows of elms fell on me, the laughter of the spring and the black chill of the night, when I a wild hunter flushed out a snowy deer; my face perished in a hell of stone.

And a drop of blood fell in the alone one's wine; and then I drank of it, it tasted more bitter than poppies; and a black cloud enveloped my head, the crystal tears of damned angels; and quietly the sister's blood trickled from a silver wound and a fiery rain fell upon me.

Along the edge of the forest I will walk, a keeper of silence from whose speechless hands the hair sun lowered; a stranger on the evening hill, who raises the lids weeping over the stone city; a deer, which stands silent in the peace of ancient elderberry trees; O restless the darkening head listens, or the hesitant steps follow the blue cloud on the hill, grim stars as well. At my side the green seedlings silently leading me on, the shy doe glides on mossy forest paths. The cottages of the village are shuttered mute and the blue lament of the wild brook betrays fear in the black wind's stillness.

But as I climbed the rock path, the madness gripped me and I screamed aloud in the night; and as I bent over the silent water with silver fingers, I saw that my face had left me. And the white voice spoke to me: Kill yourself! Sighing, a boy's shadow rose inside me and watched me shining from crystal eyes, which I lowered crying amid the trees, the enormous vault of stars.

A wandering without peace through wild rock far from the evening hamlets, homecoming herds; the setting sun grazes on a distant, crystal meadow and unsettling is its wild song, the lonesome call of the bird dying away in blue calm. But you quietly come in the night, when I lay awake on the hill, or berserk in the spring storm; and ever blacker the melancholy clouds my detached head, dreadful bolts frighten my eternal night soul, your hands tear open my winded breast.

When I walked into the garden in twilight, and the black figure of evil had yielded to me, the hyacinthine stillness of the night surrounded me; and I sailed in a crescent-shaped boat across the stagnant pond and a sweet peace touched me on the brow turned to stone; and when I died in witness, fear and that pain deepest inside me died; and the blue shadow of the boy rose lighting the darkness, a soft singing; on lunar wings, above the greening treetops, crystal cliffs, rose the white face of the sister.

Silver-footed I descended the thorny steps and I entered the lime-washed chamber. A candlestick burnt silently within and I covered my head in crimson linen; and the earth expelled a childlike corpse, a lunar thing which slowly emerged from my shadow, which down cascades of stones with broken arms, fleecy snow.

Notes

PAGE 11 | 'Dreamland, an Episode'
First published in the *Salzburger Volksblatt*, 12 May 1906.

PAGE 17 | 'From *A Golden Chalice*: Barabbas'
First published in the *Salzburger Volksblatt*, 30 June 1906.

Title, 'From *A Golden Chalice*' (*Aus goldenem Kelch*), an allusion to the Holy Grail and an overarching title to an unfinished series of prose pieces about the Passion of the Christ.

Barabbas (*Barrabas/Barrabam*), or Jesus Barabbas, a criminal figure in the Passion of the Christ who was released by Pontius Pilate at the behest of the Jerusalem mob in favour of Jesus Christ.

Oil of nard (*Narden*), an aromatic and essential oil made from the roots of the spikenard and used in balms, ointments, perfumes, incense and the like

Pearls (*Perlen*), dissolved in wine, were used in ancient times both for elevating the honour of being served the beverage and cutting any bitterness with an expensive antacid.

PAGE 21 | 'From *A Golden Chalice*: Mary Magdalene'
Originally published in the *Salzburger Volksblatt*, 14 July 1906.

Agathon and Marcellus, Greek and Roman names, respectively, suggesting that the characters, who are in love with the native Jewish women, could be soldiers or civil servants.

Hetaera (*Hetäre*), a Greek word for a courtesan, originally practised in the high arts and philosophy, that came to be applied to any prostitute who provided common entertainments such as singing and dancing.

Golgotha, Aramaic name of Calvary from the skull-pan shape of the hill.

PAGE 27 | 'Neglect'

First published in the *Salzburger Zeitung*, 20 December 1906.

PAGE 32 | 'The Morning Song'

First published in the *Salzburger Volksblatt*, 26 April 1908.

PAGE 34 | 'Dreamwalker'

First published in the *Salzburger Volksblatt*, 7 November 1908.

PAGES 35–6 | 'The Three Ponds in Hellbrunn'

First version.

First published in the *Salzburger Volksblatt*, 8 April 1909.

PAGE 37 | 'St Peter's Cemetery'

First published in the *Salzburger Volksblatt*, 8 April 1909.

Title, *St Peter's Cemetery*, located at the foot of the Festungsberg and dominated by the fortress of Hohensalzburg, the Petersfriedhof is Salzburg's oldest cemetery.

PAGE 46 | 'Three Dreams'

Line 2:4, *inexactness* (*Ungefähre*), something vague, approximate, even superficial, cf. Rilke's later usage in *Die Aufzeichnugen des Malte Laurids Brigge* (The Notebooks of Malte Laurids Brigge, 1910), in which his alter ego states 'Er war win Dichter und haβte das Ungefähre' (He was a poet and hated approximation).

PAGE 50 | 'Twilight'

Line 7, *degodded* (*entgöttert*), the word alludes to Schiller's poem, 'Die Götter Griechenlands' (The Gods of Greece).

| 'Hymn to the Night'

Line 4:2, *shed ... blood* (*blut ... hin*), the verb *hinbluten* is often used in the context of giving one's life, as in the Christ's Passion.

Line 4:8, *irreal* (*wesenlos*), a loan word in German and rendering in this way approximates the liminality and ghostliness lacking in *unreal*.

Line 8:3, *house of joy* (*Freude Haus*), cf. *Freudenhaus* (house of joys, i.e. prostitution).

| 'The Deep Song'

Title, *The Deep Song* (*Das tiefe Lied*), after the lyrics 'The world is deep . . . Deep is its woe' from Chapter 79, 'The Drunken Song', of Nietzsche's *Thus Spoke Zarathustra*.

| 'Ballad'

Line 5, *Marble Hall* (*Marmorsaal*), the name for several famous baroque ballrooms–reception halls. In the case of Salzburg's Mirabell Palace, it is a concert room.

| 'Melusine'

Title, *Melusine*, a female water spirit whose lower extremities are variously depicted as the tail of a mermaid, serpent, twin fish or a dragon. In Austrian folklore, her cries have traditionally been associated with the spring foehn wind.

| 'Outdoor Theatre'

Title, *Outdoor Theatre* (*Naturtheater*), though the title could be rendered as 'Nature Theatre' or 'Theatre in Nature', it would take away from another meaning more intrinsic, in keeping with a childhood setting and play.

| 'Coda'

Title, *Coda* (*Ausklang*), the final notes, fade out or finale of a musical piece.

| 'Crucifixus'

Title, *Crucifixus*, Gothic cross in the form of the letter Y, like the one in Cologne's St Maria im Kapitol.

| 'Confiteor'

Title, *Confiteor*, Latin for 'I confess' and alluding to the prayer said during beginning of a Roman Catholic Mass.

| 'Blood Guilt'

Title, *Blood Guilt* (*Blutschuld*), an ancient legal term for a crime involving the shedding of blood (murder), the pollution of a bloodline (incest) and hereditary guilt (e.g. the anti-Semitic notion of blood guilt for the crucifixion).

Line 9, *fountain of sirens*, and line 10, *sphinx*, in addition to their mythological connotations, these allude to sculptures in Vienna's Upper Belvedere Palace.

| 'The Saint'

Line 19, *evoë*, the traditional Greek–Latin exclamation to honour the wine god Dionysus.

Line 13, *Exaudi me* (hear me), is found in such Latin prayers to the Virgin Mary as 'Obsecro te' (I beseech thee) and 'Memorare, O piissima Virgo Maria' (Remember, O gracious Virgin Mary).

| 'De Profundis I'

Title, *De Profundis*, Latin title of Psalm 130, literally, 'from the depths'. This is the earlier of two poems that use this title.

| 'Wondrous Spring'

Title, *Wondrous Spring* (*Wunderlicher Frühling*), the adjective *wunderlich* here retains its dual and thus ironical meaning when applied to time and events, that *of wonder* and *unusual* (cf. *Annus mirabilis*, wondrous, remarkable or auspicious year).

Line 4, *three angels* (*drei Engel*), an allusion to the three angels and their final message of warning to the world in Revelation 14:6–12.

PAGE 106 | 'Lucent Hour'

Line 8, *beast with two backs* (*Tier mit zweien Rücken*), a euphemism for lovers engaged in sexual intercourse from the French phrase *la bête à deux dos* in Rabelais' *Gargantua and Pantagruel*.

Line 13, *Phoebus*, i.e. Apollo, the Greek sun god.

Line 14, *Aphrodite*, the Greek goddess of love and sister of Apollo whose incest is invented here.

Line 15, *ambergris* (*Ambraduft*), a fragrant substance produced by sperm whales used in perfume making.

PAGE 107 | 'Childhood Memory'

Line 7, *ether* (*Äther*), in addition to its literary meaning (the sky or any rarefied, ethereal realm), this alludes to sniffing ether and chloroform for their narcotic and sensory effects (one of Trakl's indulgences).

PAGE 111 | 'Colourful Autumn'

'Music in the Mirabell', first version.

PAGE 113 | 'Summer Half-Light'

Title, *Summer Half-Light* (*Sommerdämmerung*), in German, *Dämmerung* is a Janus word (i.e. a contranym), and can mean both twilight and dawn based on the quality of the daylight. Thus, this poem can be read as taking place at two different times. However, certain clues favour an evening setting and more ironic reading.

Line 2, *smell the morning* (*wittern ... den Morgen*), idiom for seeing one's chances.

PAGE 117 | 'Lamentation'

Line 1, *flutters* (*gaukelnd*), the ductile verb *gaukeln* essentially means to trick or beguile the eye with manipulation, like that of jugglers, magicians, even striptease artists and exotic dancers—such as Salome, whose presence may be intended here.

Line 6, *Kidron*, a valley and stream south of Jerusalem's Old City, the site of an ancient cemetery, the Garden of Gethsemane.

Line 7, *stellar clouds* (*Sternennebel*), although the German can be rendered poetically as *stardust*, the same word is synonymous with *nebula*.

Line 15, *murdered children*, the Holy Innocents.

PAGE 118 | 'Spring of the Soul'

Line 7, *heralding the end* (*läutet ab*), a death bell, the ringing for the last round of drinks, a departing train and the like.

PAGE 119 | 'Half-Light in the West'

Line 9, *Quirinal*, one of the Seven Hills of Rome, also the site of the Quirinal Palace, but here an analogy.

Line 20, *greyness* (*Graun*), the uncertain effect of this ductile noun allows the closure to also read 'in horror' or even 'in dawning'.

PAGE 121 | 'To Angela'

Second version.

Title, *Angela*, a female name meaning 'she who is angelic'. Like Johanna, the name appears in other poems and may be an alias for Trakl's sister.

Line 21, *Sebastian*, Trakl's alter ego in his posthumously published second book, *Sebastian Dreaming*.

PAGE 125 | 'Winter Path in A Minor'

Title, *A Minor* (*a-Moll*), in classical music, this scale is considered suitable for expressing sadness and like effects.

PAGE 127 | 'Afoot'

Second version.

PAGE 129 | 'December Sonnet'

Second version.

Line 1, *troupe* (*Gaukler*), *Gaukler* is now virtually interchangeable with the younger English word *busker* and can mean any kind of itinerant street performer, including jugglers, acrobats, magicians, shell gamers, musicians, singers, dancers, actors and so on. A literary example familiar to Trakl and his contemporaries would be Mignon and her 'gypsy' band in Goethe's *Wilhelm Meister's Apprenticeship*.

PAGE 137 | ' . . . manuscript of poems'

The following translations are of five poems attributed to Georg Trakl in Marty Bax's biography of Grete Trakl, *Immer zu wenig Liebe* (2015). All resemble poems Trakl wrote between 1909 and 1912. The manuscripts are part of the Richard Buhlig Collection, Santa Clara University Library.

The Midday

No path went to a cottage any more.
And through the grove full of silence and grief
Drove a sudden golden rain shower.
The day stood soundlessly in the midst.

The earth has drunken the ice cold water,
At the forest's edge a fire was going out,
The wind sang softly with angels' voices
And shuddering I have dropped to my knees,

In the heather, in bitter cresses,
And light and shadow were motionless;
Daedalus' ghost was on the meadow,
The sky clear and inconceivable.

The Dying Forest

A roof of branches, turned stone and grey.
In the thinning, withered maze of leaves
Flutter butterflies, drunk and mad.
Axe blows fade away in the pale blue.

In the bush burns wanton a faunlike mouth
And light and shade dance in the foliage.
For hours long falls coppery dust
Rustling in the rotten valley.

With evening icy peaks begin to glow
And the wind with a violent clatter
Laughingly thins the dying maze of leaves.
Swallows fly in a haste southwards.

Solitude

How deeply alone are house and garden!
The silver willows stand veiled along the brook.
Blackbirds intersect the blue in confusion
And sometimes the wild grass shakes in the wind.

A smell of incense floats high in the room
And a portrait watches alone in its niche,
The elder trees whisper before the window
And flood wonderfully towards the light.

A sound of horn calls fade far in the valley.
The ivy rustles upon the sandstone steps,
Where a toad sits in a squat, grey and old.

Bees very softly hum in the mignonettes.
But the red forests fall silent all around
In a sky which is without clouds and cold.

Feeling

The chemicals of rot flow into grey,
In a gold-wrought chaos of leaves,
Where butterflies flicker drunk and mad,
In incense turned yellow and lukewarm,

Bright sun seethes in the burial ground
And new sap rises up in the leaves.
I inhale the clanging and silver dust,
With the noon glowing hot and whole.

An unforeseen glow flows upwards
And wipes clean inscriptions and stones,
Which loom touchingly in wild grape,
Circled by the mosquitos' dance.

Miserables

Acres of stone, a sunlit afternoon,
Labourers' huts, gardens scorched and desolate!
Votive lights play about a steel scaffold
And hammers pound glowing white and remote

In the quarry utterly filled by red dust,
Straining arms and legs, fluttering garments.
And sometimes a hand crawls over the rock
And the sickly poplar leaves rise trembling.

Gasping women, numbers of screaming children!
O tortured cry, which swells in something gold!
A red bunting blows away in the grey.
In clouds of powder a bugle call blares.

Isles of light, flashing from heart- and hammer beat,
O yellow flame, which consumes the marrow!
Turmoil and terror race in a dull heart,
The day blurs in a haze of sweat and blood.

O seething ore, which dwells within the limbs!
O workday's end! Homecoming hard and tired!
A river, which runs filthy through the twilight.
O glowing city on the green horizon.

PAGE 139 | ['A tapestry in which the stricken landscape pales']
First version.

Line 7, *guldens* (*Gulden*), the old banknotes used in Austria-
Hungary, rendered worthless after the introduction of the crown
(*Krone*) in 1892.

PAGE 143 | ['Going Down']
First version.

PAGE 144 | 'Delirium'
Line 3, *glaciers* (*Firne*), a *Firn* is the upper part of a glacier composed of old snow. The blue colour of its ice is reflected from the sky.

PAGE 145 | 'At the Rim of an Old Fountain'
Second version.

PAGE 147 | 'Quietly'
'Melancholy', first version.

PAGE 148 | 'In the Hospital'
'Human Misery', first version.

PAGE 156 | 'Summer'
'Evening in Lans', first version.

PAGE 157 | 'December'
'On the Moor', first version.

PAGE 158 | 'Judgement'
Title, *Judgement* (*Gericht*), a double entendre in that *Gericht* can mean a delicious meal, an irony suggested in the last line.
Line 4, *Angeleus*, a Marian prayer said three times daily to honour the Incarnation.
Line 8: *Dies Irae*, a medieval Latin hymn sung during the Roman Catholic Mass for the Dead that describes Judgement Day, that 'day of wrath (*dies irae*)'.

PAGE 159 | 'Evening Glass'
'Afra', first version.

PAGE 160 | 'A Sister's Garden'
First version.

PAGE 161 | 'On the Hill'

'Ghostly Twilight', first version.

PAGE 162 | ['Hohenburg']

First version.

Title, *Hohenburg*, Schloß Hohenburg near Innsbruck, the home of the Austrian musicologist Rudolf von Ficker, where Trakl stayed as a guest in 1913 and 1914 during bouts of depression.

PAGE 163 | ['Wind, white voice, which whispers at the drunkard's temples']

Second version.

PAGE 167 | 'Wanderer's Sleep'

'The Wanderer', first version.

PAGE 168 | 'Along Walls'

'In the Dark', first version.

PAGE 169 | 'To Novalis'

First version.

Title, *Novalis*, the pseudonym of the German Romantic poet Georg Philipp Friedrich Freiherr von Hardenberg (1772–1801).

PAGE 171 | 'In the Winter'

'A Winter Evening', second version.

PAGE 173 | 'Passion'

Second version.

PAGE 178 | 'Evening Land'

Second version.

PAGE 185 | 'Melancholy'

Line 9, *pretty young girls* (*Dirne*), the remote–rural setting suggests that this term, often translated *prostitute* or *whore*, be rendered more ambiguously, for it can mean *any* young girl, promiscuous or not, and capable of being sexually desired; *dew has spilt*, idiom for ejaculation.

PAGE 186 | 'To Lucifer'

Third version.

Line 9, *eclipse* (*Finsternis*), usually rendered as blackness, darkness, gloom and the like, *Finsternis* also means this celestial event, which can be seen as one of light in the closure.

PAGE 189 | 'Over New Wine'

Second version.

PAGE 190 | 'Gloom'

Second version.

PAGE 192 | 'On'

'The Homecoming', first version.

PAGE 195 | 'Autumn Homecoming'

Third version.

PAGE 196 | 'Reverie'

Third version.

PAGE 197 | 'Psalm'

Line 18, *Mount Calvary* (*Kalvarienberg*), Trakl uses this placename in more than one poem. It may allude to both the Calvary of the New Testament and a famous hill in Salzburg.

PAGE 199 | 'Sight'

'Night Surrender', second version.

PAGE 200 | 'To the Night'

'Night Surrender', fourth version.

PAGE 201 | 'Dwindlings'

Second version.

PAGE 202 | 'Sleep'

First version.

PAGES 209 | 'Helian's Song of Destiny'

Attributed to Margarete Jeanne Trakl and located in the papers of Ludwig von Ficker, University of Innsbruck.

There will be a day full of joy
When we go stepping through the drunken grove
There will be a day full of joy
On such a day I want to set you free

And were our joy from deepest sorrow
Then shall we celebrate our high time
And were our joy from deepest sorrow
We are children of eternity

And our deepest want flowers from joy
We greet exultant the holy death
And our deepest want flowers from joy
We blaze from dawn to dawn's red sunrise

PAGE 227 | 'A Spring Evening'

First published in *Die Pforte. Eine Antholgie Wiener Lyrik* (The Portal: An Anthology of Viennese Poetry), Heidelberg, 1913.

Line 1, *larvae* (*Larven*), the Latin word in German—and even in English—imparts all of its meanings here: ghosts, masks and caterpillars—perhaps the silk tents of the common European lackey moth.

Line 5, *corn bleeds* (*Mais blutet*), a good yield, the way grain trickles (from English dialect)

PAGE 228 | 'In an Old Garden'

First published in *Ein literarisches Sammelwerk. Hrsg. von den junge Mitgliedern der Liteatur- und Kunstgesellschaft „Pan"* (A Selection of Literary Work: Edited by the Young Members of the Literature and Art Society 'Pan'), Salzburg, 1913.

PAGES 229–30 | 'Evening Reel'

Second version. The first version features a line which uses a variant of Grete ('You laugh so loudly brown Gret').

First published in the belletristic supplement of the *Die Sonntags-Zeit*, Vienna, 19 October 1913.

Title, *Reel* (*Reigen*), in its earliest form, a round or ring dance performed with joined hands and the music that accompanies it.

Line 15, *rue* (*Raute*), i.e. mignonettes, a fragrant ornamental planted outside doors and windows and believed to ward off snakes, frogs and other pests.

PAGE 231 | 'Night Soul'

Third version.

First published in *Phöbus. Monatsschrift für Aesthetik und Kritik des Theaters* (Phoebus: A Monthly Journal for Aesthetics and Criticism of the Theatre), June 1914

Line 7, *Larva* (*Larve*), see note to 'A Spring Evening'.

PAGES 233–34 | 'The Heart'

Title, *Heart* (*Herz*), term of endearment.

Line 24, *girl-youth* (*Jünglingin*), the rendering, borrowed from Victorian English, approximates the ambiguity of the German.

PAGES 235 | 'Sleep'

Second version.

PAGES 241 | 'The Despair'

Line 22, *she-monk* (*Mönchin*), the rendering is an attempt at both German meanings, the feminine form of monk (i.e. a nun) and the implicit sexual ambiguity, for the word can facetiously mean a woman cross-dressed in a habit, as in a *Mönchshure* (monk's whore), *Kirchenhure* (church whore) or *Altarhure* (altar whore).

PAGES 242 | 'The Homecoming'

Second version.

Fifth version.

Line 8, *final pulls* (*letzte Züge*), the German also means the taking of one's last breaths, a death rattle.

Second version. There is no extant copy of the first.

Title, *Grodek*, a town in eastern Galicia and a major war zone in September and October 1914, when the army of Austria-Hungary counterattacked the advancing Russian to relieve the fortress of Przemyśl.

Line 9, *lunar cold*, a full moon occurred on 4 October.

Line 14, *in the reeds*, from 'im Rohr', translated in keeping with the marshlands around Grodek.

Line 17, *descendants* (*Enkel*), a rendering influenced Derrida and Heidegger, since the war dead cannot have grandchildren (*Enkel* in the usual sense). Here the word suggests another and rarer meaning, nephews and nieces, that is, descendants or inheritors who are not directly descended from a person but from their siblings.